HOW TO BE A MORE
PERCEPTIVE DRIVER

D1316455

WARREN P. QUENSEL
Former Teacher and
State Supervisor

SAFETY ENTERPRISES
Bloomington, Illinois

ISBN 0-9636134-1-3

Printed in the United States of America

SAFETY ENTERPRISES
1010 South Summit
Bloomington, Illinois
309/828-0906

CONTENTS

Preface

While the more serious highway traffic problems are created by drunk and reckless drivers, the majority of automobile collisions are due to the occasional errors of law abiding drivers. Based on national statistics, it is estimated that at least one of every ten drivers will be involved in an automobile collision each year unless they improve their driving skills.

Why are so many drivers involved in automobile collisions, and how can we prevent them? Studies show there was some surprise on the part of one or both drivers involved. There was a lack of awareness of what was about to happen or could happen. So, we must conclude that the perceptual skills of many drivers are inadequate for operating motor vehicles.

To prevent collisions, drivers must improve their ability to observe and identify many events, from all directions, that are related to the movement of their vehicles. Since the senses of drivers are usually being exposed to more traffic events than they have time to become aware of, they must select and process only those key events which will affect their path of travel. So, the main purpose of this book is to help you learn a better process for the systematic and effective gathering of information under time restraints.

Once drivers learn how to improve their perceptual skills, they must learn how to make better responses. Too often in critical situations, drivers panic, slam on the brakes and lose control. They are not well enough prepared to cope with the complex situations they must face from time to time. So, another purpose of the book is to help you learn how to cope successfully with critical situations once they are perceived.

Our overall goal is to help reduce the enormous losses from collisions, now figured in the billions of dollars annually, due to the injuries, deaths, property damage and wasted time.

CHAPTER 1
INTRODUCTION TO DRIVER IMPROVEMENT

Driving a modern automobile presents us with an interesting paradox. To the casual observer, the ability to drive an automobile safely consists merely of applying the rules of the road and having those operating skills needed for maneuvering the automobile in traffic. In fact, this is all you need to pass the state road test. From this viewpoint, and with all the power assists now available, driving on modern highways does seem to be a rather easy task. So, before we can improve our driving skills, we must recognize that driving is a more demanding and hazardous task than most people realize. Otherwise, why are millions of experienced drivers involved in collisions each year?

The main reason driving is such a demanding and hazardous task is that it takes place in a rather complex highway transportation system. In this system, drivers operate their motor vehicles, with or without passengers, on a roadway that is part of an existing network of highways. This network has a multitude of origins, exits, geometric designs, traffic controls and facilities. The maintenance varies from state to state and city to city. Millions of drivers, each with different goals and personal traits, operate many kinds of motor vehicles in the network. People on foot or riding bicycles also use the system. The continuous interaction of these many system elements generate a countless number of traffic situations, some of which make driving a difficult task.

Based on this brief analysis of the system, it is clear that competent drivers do more than just operate and guide automobiles. They are constantly involved in processing information and deciding how to share the roadway with other users. The physical skills of driving are important, but they are easily mastered by almost everyone with little practice. The difficult part of driving is the mental ability of perceiving and then choosing the best course of action.

Fortunately, most traffic situations in the system are routine and easy to deal with. Now and then a complex situation arises which drivers must cope with in a limited amount of time. The failure of drivers to perceive and respond properly to such situations leads to most collisions.

Following are the general guidelines that have led to the developement of this comprehensive driver improvement program. They are based on two decades of teaching experiences and several driver task analysis studies. The better you understand these guidelines, the more reason you will have for practicing the specific skills and habits that are described in the rest of the book.

Use Efficient Eye Habits

Awareness is the first step in the perception process. We can't perceive something of which we are not aware. To become aware of something means we must give attention to it through our senses. The senses send the incoming information to the brain for processing. For example, we become aware of a four-legged and hairy animal through our sight. The eyes send the information about certain features to the brain, where the animal is identified as a dog. If the tail is wagging, we may identify the dog as friendly.

Your actions in traffic are mostly the result of how you use your eyes and the meaning you take from what you see. Efficient eye habits will provide you with correct and continuous observations related to the driving task. They will give you a better feeling of security and assurance. They also will help reduce mental and physical strain that can reduce the chances for fatigue. Most important, they will help you stay alert.

The warning to be alert while driving is too general and has had little effect on improving eye habits. One problem in maintaining driver alertness is that some sections of a highway can become boring. Straight, flat roads, with little traffic, can easily let your mind wander to anything other than the task at hand. This tendency can be overcome if you develop scanning habits for all roadway conditions in addition to regular mirror and dash checks. Specific scanning habits will be suggested in the next chapter.

Use a Systematic Search Pattern

It takes time for the brain to process information, though it may be only a fraction of a second. And, a car moving at high speed can still move quite a distance during this short time. In the complex highway system, our senses can send more information to the brain than can be processed in a given moment. So, in a moving car, **what we attend to and perceive must be a selective process.** Drivers without selective seeing habits are easily distracted by those events unrelated to the driving task. Then, these drivers take risks without recognizing such risks have potential danger.

To avoid collisions, your primary search of the traffic scene must be directed toward those other user actions that could result in probable conflicts within your intended path of travel. The path of travel is that strip of roadway that is wide enough and long enough to permit the safe movement of your car. It is the basic path of reference for the selection of what to perceive as well as for the guidance of your car. Anything not related to your intended path of travel should be passed over quickly. Then, you will not be distracted from perceiving the critical events.

When there are many things to observe in a limited time, it is best to deal with them in a few meaningful groups. This aids the selection process and insures that you do not overlook something critical. So, we will classify all the highway system events into three major groups. You should search first for **traffic controls,** second for **highway conditions,** and last for **other users.** We will devote a chapter to each group.

Have a Plan of Action for Choosing Responses

In driving, making choices is a continuous process. Drivers must decide how to respond to what has been perceived. They must decide whether or not they have a clear path of travel ahead for their existing position and speed. Then, for any changes identified, drivers must choose what control actions to take and the best time to respond.

Remember, mental actions do take time, even if only a fraction of a second. To make decisions and carry them out in time, you must be prepared. When you come upon a car at the side of the road, you should think about the action that may be necessary. As you spot a shaded area in cold weather, you will want to be mentally prepared for a possible slippery area. The lack of such preparation will increase the chance for error.

For you to be mentally prepared ahead of time calls for a **plan of action.** Such a plan is a set of responses that are prepared for various situations. Generally, a plan of action has to do with the proper use of time and space. It should also include the required procedures for maneuvering your car in the most favorable position for avoiding conflicts. A big advantage is that you can keep control of most traffic situations in your own hands. Then, you will be less apt to become dependent upon the skill and knowledge of other drivers and pedestrians. Three chapters will help you choose the best plans to follow.

Minimize High Risks and Avoid Them When Practical

Knowledge and competent performance are basic to safe driving, but they are not enough. Real safety requires that you have self control and a sense of responsibility at all times when behind the wheel. Risks are an inevitable part of driving, but the responsible driver does not take high or unnecessary risks.

As a perceptive driver, you can learn how to minimize the risks inherent in driving a powerful motor vehicle. In the last chapter, you will be provided with a set of strategies for assessing and managing the risks that you will encounter as a driver. When these mental strategies and habits are regularly followed, they then can become a part of your personalized and involuntary behavior patterns.

Bad habits are easy to get but hard to live with. Good habits are hard to get but easy to live with. When you choose a habit you also choose its result. The best way to change a habit is to replace it with another.

CHAPTER 2
IMPROVING EYE HABITS FOR DRIVERS

Driving an automobile is a full-time seeing operation. Developing more efficient eye habits is the first step toward improving your perceptive driving skills.

The eyes are like a camera to the brain. They first must focus on an object. Then, they take the picture for the brain to process. With central vision, your eyes can flash 30-40 pictures per second to the brain. Central vision is in focus for a clear picture because it is narrow and sharp.

Before focusing on an object, the eyes usually detect the object with fringe vision. Fringe or peripheral vision uses the upper, lower, and side parts of your eyes. It is sort of fuzzy and out of focus, but it does many important jobs for the driver. Fringe vision detects objects, movements, and shades of light all along your path of travel. When used properly, it keeps you alert and helps you select those things upon which to focus.

There are six specific eye habits which help you use both central and fringe vision efficiently. As an experienced driver, compare your present seeing habits with those described here. The objective is for these eye habits to function automatically no matter what the distraction.

EYE HABITS FOR VEHICLE CONTROL

The first three eye habits are for steering and controlling a vehicle along a given pathway. These are basic to lane control, meeting oncoming vehicles, lane changing, cornering, passing, and parking.

Picture the Intended Path Of Travel

As drivers, we guide our vehicles along selected pathways within the roadway. So, you should always have a mental picture of your intended path of travel. This gives you a target to steer toward and space to move into. It will also help you judge the best travel speed.

On many streets and highways, traffic lanes are well marked. When lanes are not marked, imagine a pathway the width of your car stretching out at least one block ahead. It is especially important to picture the turning path or the lane-changing path you expect to follow. Remember, the sharper the turn, the wider the pathway you will need.

Look Far Ahead

If you are to have enough time for making decisions and space for car control, you must be looking far ahead. The distance you look ahead is called visual lead and should be equal to at least twelve seconds.

In urban areas, a twelve-second visual lead is about one block. At sixty miles per hour on rural roads, a twelve-second visual lead is about three tenths of a mile. Use your odometer to check out how far you are looking. Pick out a fixed roadside object where you usually look. Then, read the tenths digit on your odometer. As you pass the roadside object, read the tenths digit again. The difference should be three or more.

Look Down the Middle of Pathway

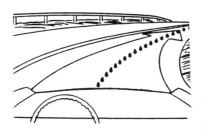

We tend to steer toward our main line of sight. So, you should use an imaginary line down the middle of your intended path of travel for steering the car. Be careful to use this center of the path only as a main point of reference. Never allow the eyes to become fixed there.

7

When you are sitting behind the wheel, there is a large area of the roadway next to your car that you can't see. This blind area in front is about fifteen feet or more, and it is greater to the rear. To your right, the blind area can be as much as one car width. So, the center of you car is best lined up with the center of the intended path of travel.

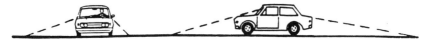

Drivers who use the right side of the road or the center line as a main point of reference usually end up with poor lane positioning and low-aim steering. When in doubt about lane positioning, use the left rear-view mirror to check how close you are to the lane line or center of the road. If space is limited on both sides, keep your car closer to the objects on the left side where small distances are easier to judge. As you begin to make turns, look "through the turn" along the projected path of travel.

SCANNING HABITS FOR THE COMPLETE PICTURE

To the eye habits for car control, you should add three habits for scanning the whole traffic scene. Continuous scanning allows your eyes to shift attention at least every two seconds. When the eyes focus on any one thing for more than two seconds, a fixed stare occurs. Then, your fringe vision will disappear almost entirely. Fixed or blank stares of more than two seconds probably trap more drivers into collisions than any other factor.

Scan the Scene Ahead and to the Sides

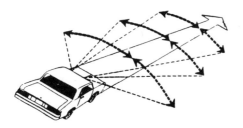

As you look far ahead for car control, use the center of the path as a point of reference for scanning from side to side. Use special search patterns at areas of

8

limited visibility, intersections, or interchanges. When following other cars, look through and around them to the second or third car ahead.

Scan the Road Surface

You should always try to scan the road surface around each object that is on or close to the path of travel. By making quick glances at the road surface, you can tell whether other drivers are maintaining good lane positions or whether a change in direction is about to take place. It will help you judge the speed and distance away of other traffic. Also, look under parked cars for signs of pedestrians.

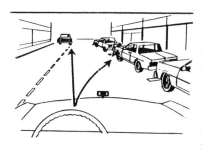 You will need to view the road surface for markings and unusual conditions. A shadow on the roadway can be a clue to a car ahead of the truck you wish to pass. Look for pot holes and slick spots, but make sure you do not focus too long on such things. Two quick looks is better than one long look.

Scan the Mirrors and Dash

Scanning the mirrors completes the circle around your car for information necessary to safe driving. The mirrors should be checked at least once every five seconds in urban areas and every ten seconds in rural areas. Mirror checks should consist of quick glances rather than one long look. Be sure to choose a safe time to look away from the roadway. In addition to the mirrors, be sure to check over your shoulder when turning and changing lanes. Remember, there will always be blind spots.

Scanning the dash is done along with the mirror checks. However, it must be done according to traffic conditions. It is usually best to check only one gauge or accessory at a time. Speedometer checks are most important when approaching curves, before exiting onto an interchange ramp, and when entering city limits. This scanning habit can help you keep your eyes moving and can be relaxing when driving becomes monotonous.

EYE HABITS FOR DRIVING AT NIGHT

Your chances of having a collision are at least two times greater at night than in the daytime. If you have an eye problem, the odds are even greater. You can be a safe driver at night if you are willing to compensate by adjusting your eye habits and speed.

How well you see at night will depend on your ability to see under low illumination, and the ability to recover quickly from glare. These abilities vary from person to person, and they decrease with age for everyone. Drivers whose eyes do not adapt well to low illumination should avoid driving at night, or at least they should limit their driving to well lighted areas.

Adapting From Light to Dark

Everyone has experienced what it is like to walk out of a brightly lighted building into darkness. Your eyes take time to adjust to such a contrast. So, when walking out of such a building to get into your car, wait at least three minutes before driving. Also, it is best to drive slowly for a few minutes. A cold engine needs a little time to warm up anyway.

When you have been outside in the bright sunshine for the afternoon, your eyes may take up to thirty minutes to adapt after the sun goes down. If you wear sunglasses, the eyes will adapt sooner. Of course, you must take off your sunglasses before driving at night.

Try To Minimize Glare

The headlights of oncoming vehicles can blind you for two or three seconds. You also can receive glare from the rear view mirror. Adjust the mirror and try never to look directly at oncoming vehicles. If you become blinded temporarily, slow down and keep right.

Modify Scanning Habits at Night

 As you approach other vehicles at night, do not continue to scan from one side of the highway to the other. Instead, use the right edge of the roadway or lane as your main point of reference. Then, scan quickly to the center of you travel path and back to the edge. Scan also from the far edge of the lighted area to near the front and repeat. It is most important that you not look to any area for more than two seconds. By using such scanning methods, you can check on the surface conditions and the relative position of the on-coming vehicles. There is always a chance a drunk driver is drifting over the center line.

SUGGESTED PRACTICE ACTIVITIES

1. When driving, have a passenger watch the inside mirror from the middle of the backseat. Within each block, the passenger is to count the eye movements to the dash and mirrors.

2. When driving at speeds up to sixty miles per hour, practice reading aloud each gauge while maintaining proper lane position.

3. In a parking lot or side street, pull up along side another car about four to six feet away. Move your car forward and backward to locate the blind spot.

4. To measure your twelve-second visual lead, pick a a fixed object ahead of where you usually look. Start counting one-thousand-one, two-thousand-two, three-thousand-three and so on until the car reaches reaches the object.

CHAPTER 3
SEARCHING FOR AND IDENTIFYING
TRAFFIC CONTROLS

When scanning the traffic scene around your car, search first for traffic controls. Controls help guide you to your destination and remind you of the rules that will get you there safely. They also will help you know what to expect of others. If all drivers better understood and followed the traffic laws, the collisions could probably be cut in half.

Traffic laws are of little value if they are not obeyed willingly and enforced strictly but fairly. The purpose of enforcement is to prevent collisions and save lives. It should never be considered as a kind of game between drivers and the police. Actually, cooperation and courtesy behind-the-wheel, if practiced regularly, would do much to reduce collisions. Courtesy in traffic probably pays bigger dividends than anywhere in every day life.

Traffic controls consist of both devices and written laws. The control devices are all those signs, signals, and markings placed on or along the roadway. Some laws, like the right-of-way, are printed in the vehicle code. So, just because there are no signs or signals present does not mean an intersection or stretch of highway is uncontrolled. All these controls are the result of years of study and experience. They are changed as a result of research findings.

As you know, traffic control devices have been de-signed with uniform shapes, colors, and symbols. This helps you identify them quickly and accurately. If you can't identify signs or signals at least ten seconds ahead, you probably need your eyes checked. The fol-lowing descriptions are for review and to help you develop a more systematic approach to the identi-fication process.

TRAFFIC SIGNS

There are four types of traffic signs. These are regulatory, warning, guide, and construction. Most signs now have symbols. With few exceptions, symbols are read from the bottom up, while word messages are read from left to right or top to bottom.

Regulatory Signs

These signs are the most important since they inform you of what can or cannot be done at certain places. Drivers who fail to follow the directions of these signs are breaking the law and can be arrested.

Three signs that regulate traffic have a red background with special shapes and deal mostly with the right-of-way. They are the eight-sided stop sign, the triangular yield sign, and the circle with a white bar. Any sign containing a red circle with a red slash means **NO.** Most other regulatory signs have a white or black background on a vertical rectangular shape. A few now may be square. These signs regulate turns, lane use, parking, and speed.

Warning Signs

These signs inform drivers about various changes ahead such as crossings, intersections, curves, changes in width, traffic conditions, and roadway conditions. They are yellow and usually diamond shaped. In general, you are to use extra caution.

There are four other warning sign shapes, each with a specific meaning. The pennant shape is for no passing. A pentagon or five-sided shape is for school zones, and the round shape is for railroads. The slow moving vehicle sign, especially for farm vehicles, is triangular with a red border.

Guide Signs

These signs are usually rectangular with the longest side horizontal. Route markers have special shapes for

County, State, U.S. Routes, and Interstates. They provide drivers with directions to places and services and other information that is not legally binding. A green background is for information about destination and mileage. A blue background is for roadside services such as food, lodging, phones, and hospitals. A brown background is for recreational and scenic areas.

Construction Signs

The fourth type of sign is for construction and maintenance areas. These signs warn of temporary hazards ahead such as slow-moving vehicles, changes in the roadway width, and workers. Recently, there has been an increase in road worker deaths, so use extra caution and always slow down. They use the same shapes and symbols as most regulatory and warning signs, but they are bright orange.

TRAFFIC SIGNAL LIGHTS

Signal lights are provided to control traffic at certain busy locations. They also indicate who has the right-of-way. You should have a clear understanding of what each color and symbol means. For example, the green light means that you may proceed with caution. It does not mean you have the right to go when a pedestrian or vehicle is still in the intersection. Make sure you know the order that signal lights flash on and off.

Standard Three-Light Control

The standard signal lights are green, yellow, and red along with walk lights. The order of the lights is: green with walk, walk off and don't walk on, green off and yellow on, yellow off and red on, red off and green with walk on. The walk lights may flash to indicate a change is coming.

Colored Arrows

You can expect green, yellow, and red arrows to be more widely used from now on. Green arrows are used to direct traffic only in the direction shown. Drivers facing a red light with a green arrow may proceed to turn in the direction of the arrow after yielding to cross traffic and pedestrians. A yellow arrow may appear after a green arrow to indicate the light will change. Red arrows prohibit traffic in the direction indicated.

Lane Signals

These signal lights are usually found hanging over traffic lanes in the city where the direction of the traffic flow changes during different hours of the day. They are also used to control traffic flow at bridges or tunnels, on expressways, and at toll booths. Be alert for the flashing yellow and red lights.

PAVEMENT MARKINGS

Lines, symbols, and lettering on the pavement are used to both warn and regulate traffic. They usually supplement signs and signals, but in some cases they are used alone. Be especially alert when the pavement is wet and icy, or when the markings are worn down.

White Lines

White lane lines are used to separate traffic going in the same direction. Broken white lines are placed on one-way streets and multiple-lane highways. Within several feet of an intersection, the broken white lines become solid. Solid white lines are also used to channel traffic in other areas. Crossing a solid white line is discouraged at all times. Double solid white lines do prohibit lane changing. Stop lines and crosswalk lines are also solid white lines.

Yellow Lines

The center lines used to separate traffic moving in opposite directions are yellow. When a broken yellow line is used on a two-lane highway, passing is permitted with due care. No passing zones are indicated by a solid yellow line on your side of the broken center line. Double solid yellow lines may be crossed only to make a left turn to or from an alley, side street, or driveway. Two-way left turn lanes in the middle of the street are marked with solid and broken yellow lines.

RIGHT-OF-WAY LAWS

The right-of-way laws may be more difficult to understand and apply because they rely on good judgement in addition to knowledge. Police report that these laws are the most difficult to enforce and issue tickets fairly. Failure to yield the right-of-way is a leading cause of collisions, many which are fatal.

Right-of-way rules are for drivers and pedestrians who wish to use the same space at the same time. The idea of right-of-way does not have anything to do with our basic rights or freedoms as individuals. They are merely rules to help drivers decide who should use the space first. Whenever you must decide who should go first, ask "Who should yield the space in the road?" So, giving the right-of-way means the same as yielding space. And remember, you have not yielded if you force another driver to slow down or wait.

Having the right to go first or to use space on the roadway does not always give one the right to take it. As drivers, we are always under the common law rule that requires us to exercise due care to avoid a crash. This means whoever has the "last clear chance" to prevent a collison should do so. Therefore, when at least two drivers approach a right-of-way situation, both should be prepared to yield. Then, in case of an error, no one will get hurt. Since anyone can become confused and make mistakes, it is well to keep in mind the following principle: "To accept a right to go first, it must first be given to you." Being lawfully right does not spare one the cost, suffering or inconvenience from a collision that results from the errors or unlawful acts of others.

DRIVER CONDITION LAWS

We all know that the physical and mental condition of a person can affect driving behavior. The motor vehicle is a machine possessing more power than is usually needed by drivers. The driver who does not have proper control of such a powerful machine can do a great amount of damage. The most serious damage can result in killing people.

Automobile homicides would normally be classified as involuntary manslaughter, since there would not be a deliberate intention to kill anyone. Because there are severe penalties for persons charged with manslaughter, the offense of reckless homicide was created with less penalties. Such homicide is still considered a serious crime and is normally classified as a felony.

Reckless Driving

According to most state vehicle codes, "a person who drives with a willful or wanton disregard for the safety of persons or property is guilty of reckless driving." Willful as used in the legal sense implies a purpose or willingness to commit an act. It implies that people know what they are doing. A wanton act is done without regard for the rights or safety of another. There is no good reason or excuse for such an act, and the person has a "don't care what happens" attitude.

Reckless driving always involves improper driving such as speeding, failing to yield the right-of-way, or a wrong turn. But, it is the conditions present and the attitude of the driver that makes the act reckless driving rather than an ordinary traffic law violation. The person who speeds through a school zone when children are present knows better.

Driving After Drinking an Alcoholic Beverage

Everyone would probably agree that a drunk person should not be allowed to drive an automobile. In fact, there has been plenty of scientific evidence collected on the effects of alcohol on driving. Therefore, all states have specific laws against driving when under the influence of intoxicating liquor. It is difficult to decide just how intoxicated a person must be before being a hazard to himself and others on the highway. How can we be sure that the behavior of a person is due to the alcohol rather than something like diabetes? Somehow it has always been difficult for people to be objective about the problem of alcohol and driving.

Fortunately, there are certain standardized tests that are accepted in the courts for measuring the amount of alcohol in the body. These tests measure the alcohol content in the blood, the breath or urine. Based on these tests, the law operates like a speed limit. When the percent of the alcohol in the blood reaches a certain level, the person is said to be legally "under the influence." If a driver refuses to take such tests, the implied consent law requires that such a person's driver license be suspended for a period of time.

These laws now make it possible to remove most of the drunken drivers from our highways. However, their enforcement is still a problem. Consuming alcoholic beverages is so common in the nation that prosecutors, judges, and juries may sometimes sympathize with the "poor guy" who got caught. So, as citizens we must all support and insist on the strict enforcement of laws that are sensible and just. Let's remember that driving is a privilege and not a right. When such a privilege is abused, it must be suspended.

Some persons may have the mistaken idea that our traffic laws limit their freedom. Actually, traffic laws promote the safe and orderly flow of traffic and still safeguard our traditional freedoms. They are based on the beliefs, behaviors, and standards agreed upon by most of the citizens. Our traffic laws can be added to or changed each time the state legislature meets. As citizens, we should understand that their effectiveness and enforcement depends mostly on our sense of responsibility, cooperation and support.

SUGGESTED PRACTICE ACTIVITIES

1. Review your official state traffic law manual for various right-of-way situations.

   a. Entering intersections with no control devices.

   b. Entering a four-way stop situation.

   c. Approaching a lane ends situation.

   d. Approaching pedestrian crossing situations.

   e. Approaching & following an emergency vehicle.

   f. Approaching & following a school bus.

   g. Approaching & following a funeral procession.

2. In urban areas, practice timing traffic lights so you can make all the green lights.

3. As a driver or passenger, use commentary driving to practice identifying traffic control devices at least one block or ten seconds ahead of your car. Compare your results with others for about six blocks at a time.

 Commentary driving consists of speaking aloud comments about what you see in the traffic scene around your car. As an example, you might make the following comments: "Speed limit is 35... My speed is 40...Open intersection... Signal light is stale green...Walk light just flashed off...My lane must turn left...No turn on red...Must yield to van...On a state highway... No passing zone ahead."

CHAPTER 4
SEARCHING FOR AND IDENTIFYING HIGHWAY CONDITIONS

Highways and streets are built, maintained, and controlled by many different political jurisdictions. As a result they differ in design features and condition. All of these differences must be identified well in advance since they can affect the movement and control of your car. A sudden change in an unfamiliar road can be quite a surprise. Since surprise is the cause of many collisions, the main purpose of the chapter is to help prevent any surprises happening to you due to the highway conditions.

A highway is made up of the roadway, shoulders, and other roadside areas usually referred to as ditches or embankments. There are many design features such as lane widths, types of surfaces, medians, curbs, sight distances, slopes, and interchanges. All of these may or may not be properly maintained.

For the safe control of motor vehicles, highways and streets should provide **adequate traction, adequate space, and adequate visibility.** But, it is the changes in these conditions that can create problems for a driver. So, we shall classify all elements or features of the highway under these three primary conditions, which must be responded to in time to avoid conflicts.

SEARCHING FOR CHANGES IN TRACTION

The control and movement of a motor vehicle depends on the friction that exists between the tires and the road surface. This friction that enables the tires to adhere to or grip the roadway is called traction. Without traction a driver cannot steer, brake, or speed up. Loss of traction means temporary loss of control which usually results in skidding.

Traction varies with the speed of the vehicle, condition of the tires, and highway conditions. Drivers can control the car speed and condition of the tires. They cannot control the highway conditions. So, you must be able to identify well in advance the condition changes. This is especially true for an area of reduced traction, since such an area usually requires a change in speed or direction or both.

An area of reduced traction is an area of the highway ahead for which the traction is less than that section of the roadway your car is traveling at the time of observation. Changes in design features, the roadway surface, and the materials on the surface should alert you to a probable area of reduced traction.

Design Features

Roadway design features in combination with other factors and forces can have a decided effect on traction. Banked and crowned roadways are especially important. A car will be much harder to control on a slick pavement that is crowned than on one that is flat. The banked roadway, usually at a curve, is also a problem.

Most highway shoulders provide less traction than the roadway surface. But, they still need to be considered an escape path. It is also possible for a car to drift off the roadway because of inattention. So, a driver should be aware of the shoulder conditions at all times.

Shoulders may be rough or soft. They are apt to have surface materials such as dirt, sand and litter. One of the most common problems with shoulders is that they are not level with the roadway. When a car drops off the roadway onto the shoulder, expect some reduced traction. Braking with two wheels on the road-way and two wheels on the shoulder will result in unequal traction and probable skidding. Then, when the car is steered back onto the roadway, the tires may slide along the edge of the pavement which creates further traction and steering problems.

Traction is affected by centrifugal force. This force creates problems when a driver is making a turn. As a car is steered around a corner, centrifugal force pulls the car outward to continue in a straight line. Traction must be great enough to overcome this force, or a car will slide to the outside of the turn.

Gravity is another force that affects traction and vehicle performance. It will affect the acceleration and speed capabilities when a car is driven up or down hills and slopes. When going up a hill the driver must accelerate to keep speed constant and overcome the force of gravity. On a slippery surface, such action may re-result in skidding due to the loss of traction. Then, when driving down a hill, the force of gravity tends to increase the speed of cars which in turn increases the stopping distance.

Slow Down

Steady

Speed Up

Surface Conditions

Traction can vary with the type of surface. A wet brick pavement or blacktop usually provides less friction than a wet concrete pavement. A bridge surface will hold frost or ice longer, especially if it is shaded from the morning sun. Chuck holes, sewer covers, drain grills, bumps, and railroad tracks all cause problems. Be extra alert for these conditions ahead of two-wheeled vehicles.

Surface Materials

Any material on the road surface can reduce the level of traction available. Look for paint, tar, wet leaves, sand, loose gravel, and mud. At intersections, oil, rubber and radiator overflow left by many vehicles starting and stopping will affect your braking distance.

Water, ice and snow usually cause the greatest changes in traction. The time and amount of water can be an important factor. At the beginning of a rain storm, the water combines with oil and dirt on the road surface to form a very slippery mixture. After a period of time, the rain washes this mixture away leaving just water. Depending on the amount of water on the surface, traction can be lost due to hydroplaning. This is the loss of traction due to the speeding tires of your car rising up on a wedge of water. It is very much the same principle that makes water skiing possible. Speed over 50 mph and worn tires are what produces hydroplaning.

SEARCHING FOR CHANGES IN SPACE TO SIDES

Drivers need adequate space for crossing, turning, merging, or for performing any other maneuver. A minimum of space around a motor vehicle also gives the driver better visibility and more time to react to the changing conditions. The amount of space required will vary with the maneuver to be made and the speed being traveled.

An area of less space to the sides is defined as a condition in which the driver does not have at least one vehicle width of open, driveable space next to the intended path of travel, or the roadway ahead becomes narrower. This could mean there will be no swerving space. These conditions are due to some change in the highway or the traffic patterns.

23

Design Features

Most changes in space to the sides are due to the design of the highway. For example, the pavement width may go from 24 feet to 20 feet, or there may be one less lane. The corner curbing may be less rounded which will require more space for turning. Then, the shoulders may become narrower.

Roadside obstructions may also reduce the space available. Guardrails, embankments, snowbanks, or rock slides may prevent you from having an escape path. There may be fencing, posts, trees, barricades, or other objects that cut down on the space available.

Traffic Situations

Other traffic on the roadway or shoulder can limit the space to sides temporarily. A line of oncoming vehicles in combination with other obstructions on the

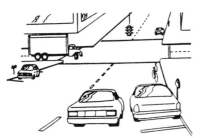

right side can limit a driver to only one lane. Cars parking or leaving parking spaces can take up one or more lanes of traffic. Pedestrians, along with oncoming cars or parked cars, will usually create space problems. Also, large trucks and buses coming or going around a corner will reduce the space available.

A combination of less traction and less space can be a most critical situation. In such areas, there is little room for correcting steering errors or adjusting speed. Only a slight side skid is enough to throw you car into a nearby object.

SEARCHING FOR CHANGES IN VISIBILITY

How well and how fast you can guide your car along the road will depend a great deal on adequate visibility. You must be able to see ahead and to the sides if you are to avoid collisions. Visibility, as used here, consists of the sight distance ahead and the field of view or the view to the sides. The line of sight is that imaginary straight line which connects the eyes with the point focused on. The field of view is the entire area of the highway that can be seen at the moment.

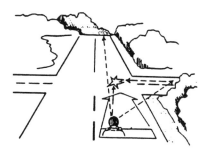 Visibility is constantly changing as you move along the highway, but it is the areas of reduced visibility that must be identified and responded to well ahead. An area of less sight distance and an area of less view to the sides shall be defined as a highway area in which the visibility ahead or to the sides is less than that required for safe travel at the speed being driven. Without an adjustment in speed, you would not be able to stop in time if another vehicle came into view. It is the same as overdriving your headlights at night.

Areas of reduced visibility may be due to weather conditions, the kind and location of traffic, conditions within you own car, and conditions of the highway. As your search for changes in visibility, ask yourself how the stopping distance compares with the sight distance. Remember, not only is your ability to see others limited, but other drivers cannot see you.

Design Features

Embankments, signs, buildings, and trees can block your view of private driveways and intersections. Hill crests and curves in the roadway can easily hide a disabled car or slow moving vehicle. Small compact cars are hidden from view by dips in the highway.

In rural areas, many side roads or private driveways may be hidden from view until you are a short distance away. In these situations, mailboxes, clouds of dust, and telephone or power lines could serve as clues to the possible presence of vehicles, animals, or pedestrians. The time of day and the season of the year should also be considered. For example, during planting and harvest time, you can expect more farm vehicles to be entering and leaving the highway. School buses can be expected at certain times and days.

Other Traffic

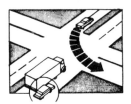

The size and position of other users can easily block your view to the sides. Large trucks and buses can reduce your view ahead. Large vehicles turning or waiting to turn can block your view to the sides.

Weather Conditions

The weather can reduce visibility as well as traction. Sudden changes in rain, snow, or fog can create some problems. The bright sunlight, when low in the sky can be a serious factor. This is especially true when the ground is snow covered.

SUGGESTED PRACTICE ACTIVITIES

1. As you drive around your community, identify situations with reduced traction, reduced space, and reduced visibility. Are these areas where collisions have occurred?

2. As a driver and passenger, use commentary driving to identify the changes in highway conditions about ten seconds ahead of your car. For example, "Curve is flat...No shoulder...Rough pavement in front of motorcycle...Less view to sides...Gravel on the pavement...Less space...Divided highway ahead."

   For the following cases, identify the important clues for changes in visibility, traction, and space.

3. Case of the Incomplete Right Turn

   On Friday about 5 pm, you are driving car "C" 25 mph on a one-way street in the business district. The car "B" driver, who is turning into a drive-in, can't complete the turn. Truck "A" is drifting toward the lane line.

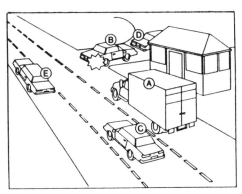

Is the time of day a factor? Will there be reduced space as well as visibility? Note the need for scaning ahead of the right turning cars as well as the roadway surface.

4. Case of the Gravel Side Road

   You are driving car "A" about 50 mph about four seconds away from a gravel side road. Car "B" has turned onto the highway. Car "C" is just coming around a curve about 50 mph and is drifting close to the centerline. Assume car "C" is about 4 seconds away from the side road.

Is traction a problem? Are there clues that would lead to reduced space and a probable conflict? Is shoulder wide enough to use as an escape path?

5. Case of the Off-Road Recovery

You are driving vehicle "A" about 50 mph on a two-lane rural highway. Car "B" has just slipped off the edge of the pavement with two wheels on the shoulder. There is at least a two inch drop from the pavement to the shoulder.

It is clear car "B" will have traction problems. What could cause a less space problem and conflict? Choices are to accelerate or slow down and steer to shoulder.

6. Case of the Windy Highway

You are driving car "B" 55 mph on a two-lane rural highway in a strong cross wind. As you approach a thick grove of trees, there is an oncoming truck.

Will there be less traction and reduced space? Then what if the road becomes slippery?

CHAPTER 5
SEARCHING FOR CLUES TO OTHER USER ACTIONS

Identifying and evaluating the actions of other users is one of the more difficult things a driver must do. Other users can travel at high speeds and make sudden changes in direction. They can start or stop quickly. The more evidence or clues you can quickly discover about other users, the better you can predict whether or not they are likely to move into your intended path of travel. The purpose of this chapter is to help you search for traffic clues in an orderly and more effective way.

QUESTIONS TO GUIDE YOUR SEARCH

The following four questions will help guide you in the search for evidence relating to other user actions.

What or Who Is It? The type of vehicle or driver will help remind you of their various capabilities and limitations.

Where Is It? This question will remind you to look for the position of other users on the highway. It is important to know whether you are in a business district, a residential area, or a rural setting.

What Is It Doing? This question will help you focus your search on the kind of maneuver another user is attempting. Then you can look for probable errors.

What Is Its Condition? This question refers to how well a vehicle has been maintained. Dirty windows and bent fenders could be clues to the other driver's visual habits or operating skills. A driver hunched over may be tired or under the influence of a drug.

SEARCH FOR MOTOR VEHICLE CLUES

You may identify a car along a curb as just parked. But, the direction of the front wheels could be a tip-off as to what might happen. If someone is in the driver's seat and the brake lights are on, you may have a possible conflict. So, when scanning the body and wheels of another vehicle, try to pick up clues that could indicate what it may do in relation to your path of travel.

Type and Condition of the Vehicle

You know that trucks, buses, and motor homes take up more space when they are turning. They usually have reduced pick-up and braking. Certain body types can create visibility problems. City buses may expect the right-of-way or take it anyway. Taxicabs may be in a hurry and take risks. Drivers of high performance cars and sport models may make quick stops, starts, and cornering maneuvers. Economy compacts can have reduced braking and pick-up capabilities.

Bent fenders and body damage could indicate a poor driver. Out-of-state license plates could mean a driver unfamiliar with the road. Glass areas partially covered with ice, snow, dirt or clothing create vision problems. An improperly or overloaded vehicle could cause steering and braking problems.

Clues to Changes in Direction

Turn signals, back-up lights, and the direction of the front wheels are obvious clues. However, some drivers fail to signal regularly, and others may forget to cancel a signal after a lane change. So, always check out the location of a vehicle on the roadway and within a lane. A car drifting toward a lane line may be starting to turn.

Clues to Changes in Speed

A puff of smoke on a moving car indicates a quick change of speed. A rapid speed-up will cause the back end to squat and the tires to squeal. Body lean on a turn may indicate speed too fast for conditions. Quick stopping actions can cause the front end to nose down.

SEARCH FOR CLUES TO DRIVER ACTION

Note the age, sex, and condition of the driver. This information, along with the condition of the vehicle, should give you an idea of the person's driving habits.

Older persons may sometimes be confused or slow to react. Younger persons may be inexperienced and apt to take more risks. A short person may have a sight problem. Others may be impaired or blinded by the sun.

Activity of the Driver

Drivers can easily be distracted by talking, smoking, eating, map reading or window shopping. If the driver is attempting some maneuver, check to see if there is enough space and time. Is the driver viewing the the scenery or tending to children? Do you have eye contact?

Common Errors to Expect

Failing to yield and failing to adjust speed are the two most common errors. Other errors involve failing to signal and failing to use the proper lane. You may also expect drivers to stop or swerve quickly to avoid some object they did not see in time.

SEARCHING FOR CLUES TO MOTORCYCLIST ACTION

Most of the collisions with motorcyclists are due to errors by the auto drivers. Because of the size and speed of motorcycles, auto drivers often misjudge the distance away. Then they fail to yield when making a left turn. Many drivers do not realize that a motorcyclist should be allowed the use of the full lane width. Never pass next to motorcycles in the same lane.

Age and Condition

 Young persons may be inexperienced and lack training. Lack of a windshield or goggles could affect vision. A passenger may affect control, especially on curves. No helmet and improper clothing may indicate a willingness to take undue risks.

Location and Activity

Note whether the cycle is close to curb, in the middle of a lane on a grease strip or to one side of the lane. Check out the condition of the pavement ahead of the cycle. Expect the stopping distance to be less than that of cars. Is it weaving, turning, or stopping? Does the passenger lean with the driver? Are there two or more cycles traveling together?

Common Errors to Expect

Since most turn signals do not self-cancel, they are apt to be left on when no longer needed. Many motorcyclists have a habit of rolling through stop signs. Some may ride on the grease strip down the center of a lane. They may ride in blind spot of cars and make quick lane changes without warning.

SEARCH FOR CLUES TO BICYCLIST ACTION

The age and size of the person could be important. Children may lack a knowledge of the traffic laws. If in a group, they may be playing and not alert to other traffic. Note whether the bike is too large for the child. The bike should have fenders and reflectors. Elderly riders may be non-drivers, have slow reactions, or be impaired.

Location and Activity

Note whether the bike is close to the curb, in the middle of the lane, or on a bike path. Rough pavement spots ahead of the bike could cause a quick stop or swerve. Remember, bicyclists must travel in the same direction as motor vehicles.

Common Errors to Expect

Many children ride facing traffic. They are apt to roll through stop signs and fail to signal. They often do not have the proper equipment and clothing for riding at time of poor visibility or at night.

SEARCH FOR CLUES TO PEDESTRIAN ACTION

Pedestrians are the roadway users most at risk in traffic. Drivers of motor vehicles or bicycles should always be prepared to yield the right-of-way.

Age and Condition

 Persons with packages or unbrellas have reduced visibility. Older persons may be impaired, have a white cane, or be a non-driver. Children are the most vulnerable and easily distracted. All persons should wear reflective clothing at night.

Location and Activity

Note whether the person is on the sidewalk, on a curb, or in the street. Is the person standing, walking, or running? Is the person entering or exiting a car? Eye contact is very important.

Common Errors to Expect

Children tend to dart out between cars and cross the street in the middle of the block. All age groups may walk against the signal light and fail to make eye contact. Adults walk when drunk.

SUGGESTED PRACTICE ACTIVITIES

1. As a driver or passenger, use commentary driving to identify the clues to other user actions at least ten

seconds ahead. Comments may include: "Parked car is backing...No eye contact with child bicyclist...Oncoming car is drifting toward the center line...Car is closing from the right...Pedestrian is off the curb...Van may not complete the turn...Ongoing car is braking...Sportscar is about to pass...Following car is tailgating."

2. After some practice, try a running commentary on traffic controls, highway conditions, and other users all at once.

3. During a period of time, keep track of the number of errors made by drivers, bicyclists, and pedestrians. Note the location of such errors.

   For each of the cases illustrated, evaluate the clues identified for other user actions.

4. Case of the Parallel Parkers

   You are driving car "A" about 25 mph in the business district. Car "C" is signaling to pull out. Drivers of both cars "C" and "D" are looking forward. Car"B" is drifting toward the lane line. Assume "B" and "E" are going about 25mph.

   How much space is needed for parked cars to exit? What action can you expect of cars "E" and "B"? Should expect a conflict in the path of travel?

5. Case of the Narrow Median

   You are driving car "A" on a four-lane divided highway. You are going 35 mph in a 40 mph zone. Car "C" is turning left, and you are not turning.

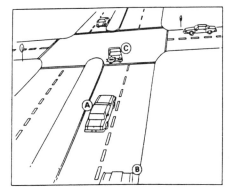

With such a narrow median, what can be expected of car "C"? Will car "B" and the side street car be a problem? What are your options?

6. Case of the Right Shoulder Hazard

You are driving car "A" on a four-lane divided highway with wide shoulders. You are starting to pass car "B". Suddenly, without signaling, car "B" swerves into your lane to avoid vehicle "C".

Was this a poor place for passing to take place? What clues should you be looking for? What are your options?

7. Case of the Supermarket Shopper

You are driving car "A" about 30 mph in a business district. You can see that car "B" will not be able to complete the turn because car "E" is backing out. Cars "C" and "D" cannot see car "E". It appears car "C" is following about two seconds from car "B". Also, car "D" is driving in the blindspot of car "C".

Will cars "C" and "D" expect car "B" to complete the turn or parking manuever? What clues should you look for? What options do you have?

8. Case of the Blocked Left Turn

You are driving car "A" at 25 mph about a half block from the corner. The signal light has just turned green. Car "B" is turning left. Car "C" is following you in the left lane.

Does this show the need to look through the turning path of other vehicles as well as your own? As driver of the following car "C", what clues would you look for?

9. Case of the Right Turn Hazard

You are driving car "A" and plan to turn right. There are drivers in both cars "B" and "C". The wheels of these cars are turned out toward the street. Also, assume you could be driving car "D" and getting ready to turn right. Are there special problems related to the parked cars at the end of the block or the beginning of a block?

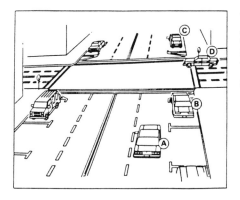

What more clues do
you need for a real
conflict to occur?
What are your
options?

10. Case of Being Passed

You are driving car "A" on a two-lane highway.
Car "C" has just passed you and returned to right
lane. Suddenly you notice car "B" is also trying
to pass. It is obvious "B" will not be able to
complete the pass before clearing car "D".

What does the law
require of driver
being passed?
What clues will
you look for?
Should you let "B"
make the first
move? What is
your response?
What would you
do as the driver
of car "D"?

CHAPTER 6
SEARCHING FOR AND IDENTIFYING CONFLICT PROBABILITIES

Traffic collisions happen because two or more users try to use the same space at the same time. These collisions can be prevented if the point of conflict is identified soon enough for one or both users to make the proper changes in speed or direction or both. This involves a driver's ability to evaluate all of the information perceived from the traffic scene. So, the purpose of this chapter is to help you improve your ability to judge what other users will do.

IDENTIFY THE THREE PARTS OF THE TRAVEL PATH

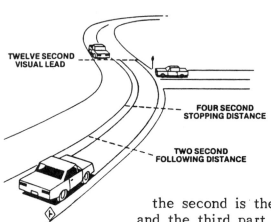

TWELVE SECOND VISUAL LEAD

FOUR SECOND STOPPING DISTANCE

TWO SECOND FOLLOWING DISTANCE

To help judge whether or not you have a clear path of travel, you should first picture the intended path of travel as being made up of three parts. The first part is the following distance, the second is the stopping distance, and the third part is the sight distance or visual lead. These distances will vary with the size and capability of your vehicle. They will also vary with the weather and roadway surface conditions.

The Two-Second Following Distance

The following distance is that space interval you should follow behind an ongoing vehicle. It is the minimum time or space needed to see, react, and brake to stop when necessary. For bad weather, poor visibility, or night driving, add one second. Also, add one second when following motorcycles and small compact cars. Add at least four seconds when the roads are covered with ice or packed snow.

To establish the two-second following distance, first pick a fixed checkpoint along the road ahead. This may be a sign, a post, a tar strip or any other fixed object. Then, start counting the seconds as soon as the rear end of the vehicle ahead reaches your checkpoint. Count one-thousand-one, two-thousand-two, and so on. If you reach the checkpoint before finishing the two-second count, you are following too close.

The Four-Second Stopping Distance

For most cars, the minimum stopping distance is the equivalent of about four seconds. This is the distance you will need to stop for a fixed object in the roadway or for traffic moving across your travel path. Add at least one second when the pavement is wet. For snow packed or icy pavements, add at least four seconds. You should never allow another vehicle or pedestrian to move into or remain in this stopping zone. You can establish the four-second stopping distance by mentally doubling the following distance or by using the counting method.

Twelve-Second Visual Lead

A distance ahead equal to twelve seconds should be considered the minimum visual lead or sight distance you will need at all times. This will give you time to perceive and decide what to do before your stopping distance is reached. Twelve seconds of distance in the city is about one block. On the highway, it is about one quarter of a mile.

IDENTIFY OTHER USER ERRORS

Very few collisions happen that don't involve human error. All drivers and pedestrians are bound to make mistakes from time to time. However, it is our responsibility to make as few errors as possible. We will make fewer driving errors and avoid the errors of other road users if we know what errors to expect. Following are examples of errors you can learn to expect and protect yourself against.

Fails to Observe Traffic Laws

The actions of drivers who know and follow the traffic laws are usually easy to detect. Look for clues to indicate that a law will not be obeyed. Most mistakes involve the right-of-way and speed laws. Some drivers run the red light or jump the green light. A common mistake involves not yielding to the car on the right. Many drivers fail to adjust their speed for the conditions.

Makes Improper Responses to Highway Conditions

Use your knowledge of highway conditions to judge what other drivers may do when faced with areas of less traction, less space, and less visibility. Are there clues the other driver does not perceive the condition? Are there clues the other driver may lose control and move into your path of travel? Will one driver force a second driver to swerve into your path?

Misjudges Distances or Space Requirements

When other drivers are attempting certain maneuvers, a common mistake is to misjudge the space needed. Therefore, you will need to be alert for the driver who tailgates, is not in the proper position for a turn, who has not allowed enough gap in traffic for a lane change, or who misjudges the space needed for passing. You can expect some drivers to misjudge the space needed for accelerating onto an interstate.

Makes Improper Car Control Responses

Some drivers tend to panic and swerve or slam on the brakes to avoid a problem they did not see in time for a proper response. Be alert for a driver who is trying to avoid a pedestrian, a slow moving farm vehicle, parking vehicles, or a driver who can't complete the turn.

IDENTIFY LOW OR HIGH CONFLICT PROBABILITIES

To avoid collisions, your search and evaluation must be directed primarily to those other user actions and road conditions that could result in movements toward your intended path of travel. The chance for other users to move into your twelve-second path of travel will be called conflict probability. Some of these movements may have a high probability for conflict, which are critical and must be responded to. Other movements may have only a low probability for conflict and usually will not require action on your part.

The best way to identify conflict probabilities is to collect evidence (clues) for or against the conflict to take place. In some cases, the amount of evidence may not be as important as the kind or quality of the evidence. The evidence can be collected when you are searching for traffic controls, highway conditions, other user actions, and probable errors of others. By using the perceptual skills learned in the last three chapters, you can be confident no probable conflicts will be overlooked.

Identify a High Chance of Conflict

A high chance for conflict is one in which there is clearly more evidence for a conflict to take place, within twelve seconds ahead, than there is against such a conflict. If there is some doubt as to a probable conflict, usually it is safest to assume the worst and predict a conflict in your path of travel. A good example would be a parked car with a driver, the front wheels turned out, and smoke coming from the exhaust. A child looking away and running toward the street would be another example.

Identify a Low Chance of Conflict

 A low chance of conflict is one for which there is very little, if any, evidence for another user to come close to your twelve-second path of travel. A pedestrian walking away from the street or a parked car with no driver would be good examples. In another situation, a car is crossing your pathway ahead, but the crossing is taking place more than twelve seconds ahead.

IDENTIFY THE PROBABLE POINT OF CONFLICT

Once you have predicted a high chance for conflict, you will need to identify when and where such a conflict would likely happen. This can be done with the evidence used for judging that a conflict is probable. The identification will involve making a judgment of the speed the other user is closing on your pathway and the amount of space the other user will take.

Judge the Speed of Closing

What is the speed of the closing vehicle or pedestrian? How fast another user is closing on your path will determine when it could reach your car. You will want to look for clues that may indicate an increase or decrease in speed. This is why timing is such an important part of safe driving.

Judge the Amount of Space Required

Some of the other users may use all of your path of travel; others may use only a part. A parallel parking car will swing into part of the second lane. Pedestrians, bicyclists, and motorcyclists very seldom take up more than a part of a standard lane width. Ongoing cars that are turning left or right may not complete the turn and still be in part of the pathway. A disabled car may still be partway on the roadway. Some of these situations may tempt drivers to just squeeze by.

SUGGESTED PRACTICE ACTIVITIES

1. As a driver or observer, use commentary driving to indicate whether or not the twelve-second path of travel is clear or not clear. Identify any probable points of conflict.

   Study and identify the probable conflicts in the following cases. These should help program your mind for dealing with actual situations.

2. Case of the Side Road Hazard

   You are driving car "A" on a two-lane highway. You have just started to speed up and pull up along the side of vehicle "B" to pass. All of a sudden, car "C" turns onto the highway from a side road.

What are the legal responsibilities of vehicle "B"? What clues should you look for? What are the options of the three drivers?

3. Case of the Squeeze Play

You are driving car "A" downtown on a four-lane undivided street. In the next block the street narrows into two lanes for traffic. Car "C" has no signal on and is centered in the lane.

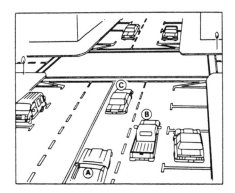

Is this a right-of-way situation? Will the parked car across the intersection be stable? Look for clues as to what "B" will do. Where is probable point of conflict?

4. Case of the Right Turn Surprise

You are driving car "D" about 55 mph on a two-lane highway. The oncoming car "B" had plenty of time to pass truck "A" and pull in behind car "C". However, car "C" slows down and starts to make a right turn with a late signal. Car "B" starts to swerve toward your lane. Also, assume you are the driver of car "B".

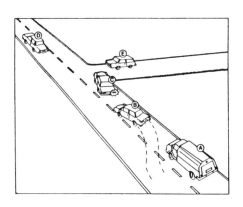

Passing near side roads creates problems, especially if there is no clear view. Should you steer to shoulder, and when?

5. Case of the Blocked View

You are driving car "A" and following car "B" at an interchange. Car "B" cannot see the merging traffic, and may not see truck "C" signals for a lane change.

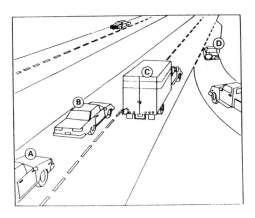

Car "B" is in the blind spot of "C" in a critical area. What clues will you look for? What is probable point of conflict, and what are your options?

6. Case of the Late Exit

You are approaching an interchange in vehicle "A". You start to exit behind car "B" who is trying to enter the freeway. All of a sudden, car "C" pulls in front of car "B" to make a late exit. Car "B" slams on the brakes.

Are there following vehicles? What are clues to the pathway car "B" will take? What is the point of conflict and your options?

CHAPTER 7
CHOOSING THE BEST PATH OF TRAVEL

Once you have perceived the changing highway and traffic conditions, you must decide how to respond. For each situation or problem faced, you should choose the best path of travel. Then you must communicate and time your actions. The best path of travel is the one that is free of conflicts at the time you will want to use it.

GUIDELINES FOR CHOOSING THE BEST PATHWAY

The best path of travel is one that provides adequate space, adequate visibility, and adequate traction.

Select a Pathway With Space Margins to the Sides

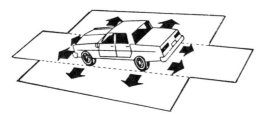

The best way to minimize hitting something or being hit is to maintain a margin of space around your car. It will provide good visibility and swerving space when needed. Always try to allow one car width of space on at least one side. When practical, keep space margins on both sides. In heavy traffic, when it is not possible to have an adequate space on either side, allow more space to the front.

Select a Pathway with the Best Visibility

A clear view ahead will give you the best chance for maintaining a steady speed. You also will be better able to identify probable conflicts early enough to avoid them. The greater distance you can see ahead, the more time you will have for adjusting your speed and position.

Select a Pathway with the Best Road Surface

There is little difference in traction for the various types of paved roads when they are dry. It is what is on the surface and the condition of the pavement that can make a difference. Pot holes, bumps, and loose materials can cause the control problems.

CHOOSE BEST LANES ON MULTIPLE-LANE ROADS

You are expected to maintain good lane control. Drifting, weaving, or straddling lane lines is the mark of a poor driver.

Following and Meeting Other Vehicles

On multiple-lane rural highways, it is best to keep to the right except to pass or turn left. Slower moving traffic may be required by law to keep right.

On urban roadways with three or more lanes going your way, choose the center lane for going straight ahead for any distance. Then, you won't be delayed by ongoing cars turning or parking. Remember that parking vehicles will use more than the first full lane for entering and exiting parallel parking spaces. Be alert for special lanes that are reserved for buses and car-pool traffic.

Turning at Intersections

Select the proper lane well in advance of the solid lane lines. Center you car in the lane so you have some space margin on each side. When stopping behind other vehicles, allow a space ahead of about five feet. If the ongoing vehicle starts up and then stops suddenly, you will have plenty of distance to stop.

When making a left turn against traffic, pull into the intersection to establish your position. Keep the front wheels straight until the turn can be completed. Otherwise, a following car may push you into oncoming traffic. If there are two or more turning lanes, always stay centered in the same lane for the full turn.

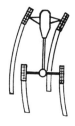

Before turning right, position your car three feet from the curb. The width of the path required to turn will depend on your vehicle length and the sharpness of the curb. The pathway must be wide enough to allow the rear wheels to track inside those of the front wheel tracks. The sharper the curb, the wider the pathway needed.

CHOOSE THE BEST POSITION WITHIN A LANE

Once you have selected the best lane for travel, then choose the best position to take within the lane. Visibility ahead and space margins to the sides are the main factors to consider.

Get into the habit of looking around, through and under other vehicles ahead. Move to one side for a better view ahead or behind. The trick to making good time in traffic is to watch ahead for tie-ups so you can choose the best free-flowing lane.

Picture Five Positions

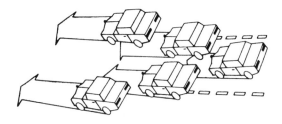

Most marked lanes are 10-12 feet wide. Since your car is about six feet wide, you can picture in your mind about five positions to choose from. If there are no lane lines, imagine these five positions about one-half car width from each other.

The center of the lane is the normal driving position. Moving one-half car width to the right or left will position your car next to the lane lines. On full car width to the right or left is the position where your car is straddling a lane line. Moving farther left or right is considered a lane change.

Positioning for Hazards to the Side

It is best to allow more distance from a hazard to one side. As an example, when approaching a vehicle parked on the shoulder, move away at least one-half car width. In rural areas, be alert for mail boxes or utility lines perpendicular to your highway. These could be clues to a hidden driveway or side road. Remember, it will take some time for a vehicle to pull onto your road and reach the speed of traffic.

When you come to an area with hazards on both sides of the highway or lane, move closest to the side with the least probable consequences. It would be best to keep more distance from a child pedestrian than from another car on the other side.

Positioning for Surface Conditions and Hills

Pot holes, gravel, or icy spots are surface conditions that can affect the control of oncoming vehicles as well as your car. Motorcyclists will have the greatest problem. Remember, frost or ice are slow to melt on bridges. Shaded areas on a cold morning could still be slippery. Crosswinds can push vehicles sideways. So, when approaching such areas, keep to that side or your lane from which the crosswinds are coming.

When practical, try to steer around areas with surface problems. When steering is not practical, use the brakes before reaching the area. Braking on such surfaces will usually cause skidding and loss of control.

When coming to a hill crest, keep close to the right edge of the pavement. Be alert for slow moving farm vehicles ahead or oncoming cars that are trying to pass.

Positioning at Curves

When approaching a curve you cannot see around, observe the line of trees or utility lines for a clue as to the sharpness of the curve. For curves to the right, enter near the center line as shown. This gives you a better view around the bend and helps you flatten out your path a little. Note that you will then have more distance from the center line at the sharpest part of the curve.

When approaching a curve to the left, you should enter closer to the edge of the pavement for the best view. Try not to meet another vehicle, especially a truck, at the sharpest part of the curve. Be alert for a motorcyclist who may be leaning near or over the center line.

CHOOSE THE BEST COMMUNICATION

Whenever you plan to change direction, other users should be told about it in advance. As a driver, you need to know if your signals are being received and heeded. Too many drivers make the false assumption that just because they have signaled, the other user has received it. Communication means exchanging information with other people. It means receiving as well as giving information.

Be a Receiver and a Sender

A driver or pedestrian should be both a sender and receiver. As a sender, you must choose the best time and method for sending the message. As a receiver, you must be able to read the messages being sent by the other person. Part of these messages should consist of feedback concerning whether or not the message was received. Some drivers count at least five clicks of the turn signal before changing lanes. They give the other drivers time to receive and react to the message. There are four types of messages to choose.

1. Intentions...I plan to turn left...I am turning here ...I am slowing down...I want to pass, move over ...I wish to back up.

2. Warnings...There is trouble ahead in my lane...I must stop suddenly...There is danger in your lane ...Your lights are blinding me.

3. Presence...I am over here...Notice me...Do you see me...I am parked.

4. Feedback...I see you...I get the message...I am waiting for you...Go ahead...I'll stay put...Thanks for helping me pass.

Methods of Communication

- Use electric or hand signals. You have a choice of turn signals, brake lights, back-up lights, and the four-way flashers.

- Use the horn. Choose a gentle tapping, a sharp blast, or a steady blast.

- Use body actions and gestures. You can use hands, make head checks, nod head up and down, smile, or look puzzled.

- Use your headlamps. You can flash headlights off and on, or you can switch them back and forth from low to high beam.

- Signaling others to pass is dangerous as well as illegal in many states.

SUGGESTED PRACTICE ACTIVITIES

For each case, judge where or when a probable conflict would occur. Then select the best lane to take and choose the best position to take within the lane. Also choose the best communication.

1. Case of the One-Way Turn Off

You are driving car "A" on a one-way street and

plan to turn left onto a two-way street. The signal
light is green. Cars "B" and "C" are going straight.

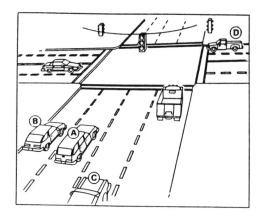

What traffic laws
apply? What clues
to driver action
should you look
for? What are the
best responses?

2. Case of the Angle Parker

You are driving car "A" in a business district.
Car "B" will not be able to complete parking without backing up first. Car "D" is tailgating and
car "E" is driving in the blindspot of car "D".

How do you expect
cars "C", "D", and
"E" to respond to
the problem of
car "B"? What
should you do?

3. Case of the Turning Truck

You are driving straight ahead in car "A". It would
appear truck "B" is turning into a two-lane side
street with traffic present. You will probably have
reduced space and visibility.

Can you expect the truck to swing into part of your lane or stop before completing the turn? Should you warn any following vehicles? What is the best postion?

4. Case of the Busy Ramp

You are driving car "A" on an interstate. Car "B" is speeding up to merge onto the freeway. There is a line of cars waiting to merge.

Do both cars "A" and "B" have a responsibility to adjust position and speed? Should a perceptive driver changed lanes sooner?

CHAPTER 8
CHOOSING THE BEST SPEED FOR CONDITIONS

Speed of movement is important to the operation of our highway transportation system. The faster motor vehicles can move safely, the more efficient the system. But, speed too fast for conditions is reported consistently as a leading cause of most collisions. The severity of collisions is also in proportion to the speed at the time of impact.

Since speed is so relative, deciding how fast to go calls for good judgment. To make such judgments, requires a set of guidelines or standards. This chapter will provide you with adequate guidelines for choosing the best speed.

THE EFFECTS OF SPEED ON DRIVERS AND VEHICLES

Humans and machines do have limitations. So, when it comes to speed control, you first should realize that high speed does affect the capabilities of both drivers and motor vehicles.

High Speed Affects Driver Capabilities

The faster you drive, the more your field of view and eye movement is reduced. At 60 mph, your field of view is less than half as wide as when you travel 30 mph. What you see to the sides may become distorted or blurred. Speed increases eyestrain, and sustained high speed dulls your sensitivity to the rate of movement.

The faster you drive, the slower your reaction time. Once the eyes send information to the brain, the brain must process the information for a decision. Then the brain causes the body to react. The more choices you give to the brain, the more time is needed to pick the best choice. For example, when you look at a traffic sign, you may not "see" it if the brain is overloaded.

High Speed Affects Vehicle Capability

As you select the proper speed to drive, you also must take into account the effect of speed on your vehicle's performance. It is obvious that the faster the speed, the further the stopping distance. What many drivers don't realize is that as speed is increased, the ability to steer sharply is reduced. Then, there is less potential for rapid acceleration when needed.

High Speed Affects Vehicle Condition

Driving at sustained high speed will cause the engine to vibrate and work harder. This leads to over-heating and less pick-up. The brakes and tires also generate heat which can lead to brake fade and a tire blowout. In addition to reduced performance, there will be higher maintenance and fuel costs. So, smart drivers will consider the high speed capability of auto engines as reserve power for use only in case of an emergency.

TRAFFIC LAWS FOR SPEED CONTROL

Based on driver limitations and many studies, traffic engineers have developed our current traffic laws. Experience has shown that speed limits are necessary for the safe and efficient movement of traffic. After all, as people drive on a specific highway for the first time, they certainly can't know the kind of conditions that lie ahead.

Maximum and Minimum Speed Limits

The fixed, or absolute, speed limit laws establish the maximum speed drivers may travel on most urban and rural highways. These laws are closely related to the natural laws of physics. It is not how fast one can go, but how fast one can stop. It may seem as easy to slow down as to speed up, but it isn't. Our traffic engineers know how many feet it takes for a moving car to stop. They also know how much centrifugal momentum a car has and the force of impact at various speeds. Sight distances and traction requirements are also taken into consideration. This is why 70 mph is the proper speed limit for our most modern interstates.

Speed Zoning Laws

All states have legislation which gives the proper authorities the right to determine whether or not a certain stretch, or zone, of roadway should have a different speed limit from that which has been set state wide. These zone limits can be set only on a basis of an official engineering and traffic investigation. Then, appropriate signs are erected and the limits enforced.

Drivers today must be more alert for work zones because there has been an increase in the number of deaths and injuries to maintenance and construction workers. For some reason, many drivers are not obeying these temporary speed limits. Proper maintenance and road improvements should be expected, and there must be greater protection for these workers.

There is a tendency on the part of we citizens to make laws, to appoint people to enforce these laws, and then to take exception for our need to obey all of the laws. Perhaps too many of us consider traffic laws as minor or "little" laws that we need not respect so much. Then, it is easy to have little sense of moral obligation to obey such laws when compared to other more important restrictions.

The Basic Speed Law

The most important and basic speed law forbids driving at a speed that endangers the safety of people and property. The key idea is that a person should always drive at a "reasonable and proper speed for the conditions." It is a rule of common sense and safety that applies regardless of the posted speed limits.

A reasonable and proper speed for any conditions is

one at which the driver can have an "assured clear distance ahead" at all times. If the speed is too fast for conditions, the driver cannot stay on the intended path of travel or stop in time to avoid a collision. Speed too fast for conditions by one driver also makes it most difficult for other drivers or pedestrians to respond properly. Following are some specific guidelines to help you select the best speed for conditions.

ADJUST SPEED FOR THE TIME NEEDED

Time is one of the most important requirements for safe driving. In a moving car, you must have time to perceive what is going on around you and then make the proper response. If your speed is too fast for the response time needed, it is obvious you will have a serious problem.

Time is Needed to Observe and Process Information

Experiments have proven that the average person can collect five to seven bits of information with each glance or eye fixation. The amount of time required for collecting information about a traffic situation depends on how many bits are to be observed. For example, it may take several glances or eye fixations to "read" overhead signs, roadway markings, and to note what other users are doing. So, speed must be adjusted to the amount of information that must be observed and processed.

Once information is sent to the brain, it must be processed and a decision made. Generally, the minimum amount of time for such a decision is about one-half second. If a driver is flooded with more information than can be processed in a given moment, mistakes are bound to happen. Remember, at 60 mph, you will travel about 90 feet in one second or about five car lengths. And after the decision is made, you still must take the car control actions.

Time is Needed for Vehicle Control Actions

To control the speed and position of your car, you must make proper use of the steering wheel, gas pedal, and brakes. You also may need to change gears, signal and use various safety devices. Operating these controls takes time, if only a fraction of a second. Then, it takes time for these control systems to respond to your actions. Altogether, these actions usually take at least one-half second while the car continues to move.

Time is Required for Making Maneuvers

Changing lanes, turning corners, merging onto the freeway, and passing all take time. Depending on conditions, these actions can take 4-10 seconds. The closer you must get to other objects, the slower the speed. This is especially true when coming close to pedestrians or slow moving vehicles, because they can stop or change directions quicker than you can.

ADJUST SPEED FOR TRAFFIC CONDITIONS

The types, the numbers, the location, and the speed of other traffic are factors that you must consider when choosing the proper and reasonable speed.

Adjust Speed for the Type and Amount of Traffic

Is traffic getting heavy? Are there trucks, school buses, two wheelers, or overloaded vehicles present? During late afternoon hours, drivers may be tired or in a hurry, and children are getting out of school. Late at night, drivers may be sleepy or under the influence of alcohol.

Farm vehicles and other slow-moving traffic present a special problem. They not only move slower, but they can be expected to turn suddenly onto or off of a side road that may be hidden from view. In farming areas, special caution is needed at dusk, since many tractors may have inadequate lights.

Adjust Speed to the Flow of Traffic

Smart drivers adjust speed to the flow of traffic or the common speed. Studies show that cars traveling 10-15 mph above or below the common speed have most of the collisions. The larger the difference in speed of moving vehicles, the greater the chance for conflicts and errors in judgment. The high speed driver is forced to weave in and out of traffic almost constantly. Blending with the flow of traffic is not only safer and more efficient, but it will save gasoline and money on maintenance.

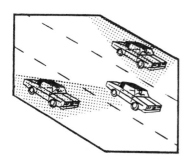

When practical, avoid driving in bunches or the blindspot. Adjust your speed to work your way through a bunch or drop back some distance from the pack if they are going the speed limit. If you must drive side by side with other vehicles during rush hour traffic, allow increased space from the vehicle ahead. Adjust speed to avoid driving in the blindspot of another driver, and do not let another driver stay in your blindspot.

Adjust Speed for an Adequate Following Distance

An adequate following distance lets you smooth out your driving. It helps you spot traffic tie-ups well ahead, and allows for more gradual lane changes. Remember, it is the space ahead of your car that you have the most control over.

Although the two-second following distance is adequate under normal conditions, you should increase the following distance behind large trucks, buses, and campers that may block your view. Keep an increased distance from motorcycles and compact cars that can stop in shorter distances. Don't forget that trucks carrying explosives or flammable liquids are required to stop at railroad crossings just as buses do. Remember to stay at least 500 feet behind emergency vehicles. Keep a greater distance from a car ahead which is tailgating the second car ahead. Any vehicle turning right should require a greater following distance. Then you are prepared to stop for an incomplete turn.

ADJUST SPEED FOR HIGHWAY CONDITIONS

A change in highway conditions is another important factor that determines whether or not a speed adjustment is necessary. It must first be assumed that a driver has selected a safe speed for the existing conditions. Then, if there is a change in these conditions, it is only sensible to decide what adjustment to make. The kind and rate of these changes is the basis for the amount of speed adjustment. Changes in visibility, traction, and space are the three highway conditions you will need to make speed adjustments for.

Adjust Speed for Changes in Visibility

The distance you can see ahead must not be less than the distance needed to stop. By law, this is the assured clear distance ahead. So, your speed must be directly related to your sight distance ahead. It is obvious for speed to be adjusted for hills and curves. What many drivers overlook is the need to adjust speed for sunglare, rain, fog, and darkness.

As your speed increases day or night, your field of view to the sides and your eye movements become quite restricted. At high speeds, this leads to tunnel vision and eye strain. So, as highway conditions change your view to the sides, there must be adjustments in speed. The loss of clues due to blurring at the sides may lead to overconfidence and even greater speed.

Adjust Speed for Changes in Traction

There is little difference in traction for the types of paved road surfaces when they are dry and smooth. Pot holes and rough surfaces can lessen traction, and crowned or banked surfaces can offer less stability than flat surfaces. But, it is what is on the surface of the pavement that causes the most change in the amount of traction. Speed adjustments for these changes is critical for steering control and adequate braking.

The least amount of traction available is on ice and packed snow. Some people have the mistaken idea that it becomes more slippery the colder it gets. Actually, the least traction for driving is when the temperature is just about freezing. This is when the surface starts to melt. The combination of water and ice becomes much slicker than dry ice. Drivers should reduce their speed by half on packed snow and slow to a crawl on ice.

Traction can be a problem on hills and curves. When approaching a curve, adjust speed to the sharpness of the curve. Also, take into account the amount of luggage and passengers in your car. Then, maintain slight pressure on the gas pedal for better traction around the curve.

Adjust Speed for Changes in Space to Sides

When you are approaching an area of reduced space on the sides, and there is little or no swerving space, a speed adjustment is your only choice. If you have poor visibility or poor traction along with limited space, a speed adjustment of the correct amount is critical.

You have no control over road conditions or the movement of other traffic. What you can control is where and when you meet other users. This is done by adjusting your speed and thus timing your car's movement. The adjustment of speed is used throughout this chapter because good timing may require acceleration or deceleration.

In the situation illustrated, you should adjust your speed so that you will not be opposite the bike rider or the car with a flat tire when you meet an oncoming vehicle. Serious consequences could arise if there were even a slight error in judgment or if the bike rider happened to veer left to avoid something in or on the pavement. It is obvious this situation should have been identified as an area of less space to the side some distance ahead.

Other examples of timing situations are as follows:

-- Try to avoid meeting large vehicles at areas of reduced space such as bridges or culverts.

-- Try to avoid meeting other vehicles at slippery areas such as shady spots and frost on bridges during cold weather.

-- Try to avoid meeting other vehicles opposite areas with strong crosswinds.

-- Try to avoid meeting other vehicles opposite a child playing nearby.

ADJUST SPEED FOR DRIVER CONDITION

The speed limits and stopping distances provided are based on the assumption that drivers are reasonably alert and have normal reaction times. There are many temporary conditions that may substantially increase your reaction time. When you are feeling good, both physically and mentally, don't you perceive the world differently than when you are tired or sick?

Adjust Speed for Fatigue

There are two types of fatigue that can affect the physical and mental condition used in driving. One is due to the lack of rest and sleep. The other is called operational fatigue. This latter condition results from continuous hours of driving without stopping. It is due also to fighting heavy traffic and bad road or weather conditions. Under these conditions, you may become irritable and over react to problems.

When you must drive long distances, plan to make regular rest stops at least every two hours. At night, a good time to stop would be your regular bed time. Your body is used to sleep then, so at this time you will get tired quicker. Always get some exercise each time you stop and avoid eating heavy foods.

If you should get real drousy, take a short nap. Then, wash your face with cold water. Some drivers fight to stay awake, and they may resort to "stay awake" pills. This makes matters worse, because when you force a tired body to stay awake with drugs, serious problems result. As the effects of the drug wears off, you fall asleep without any warning.

In addition to adjusting speed, change your seat position from time to time. Open a window or vent for fresh air. Talk about the trip plan and take turns driving. If you are alone, sing occasionally, chew gum, and always keep your eyes moving.

Adjust Speed for Emotional Upsets

All drivers are subject to emotional upsets before or during a trip. Before driving, a person may have had a stressful day at work or may have become upset at something or someone. While driving, a person may get angry at other drivers for their errors.

Strong emotions usually have a profound effect on behavior. Besides the effect on one's perception and judgment, they cause bodily changes in breathing, blood pressure, and muscle tenseness. These changes call for speed adjustments. In extreme cases, a driver should stop and wait for the emotion to subside to a safe level.

Adjust Speed for Temporary Illnesses

Everyone suffers from colds, headaches, or the flue from time to time. Many people are affected by hay fever and other allergies. Most of these temporary illnesses probably affect our visual efficiency first. There also may be various degrees of dizziness, pain, or nausea. These conditions make it difficult to keep your mind on driving. As a result, your timing and coordination can be affected.

The drugs taken for illnesses may have more effect on driver ability than the illnesses themselves. This is due to the side effects that some drugs have on the body. Many people take drugs for weight reduction, high blood pressure, diabetes, and other permanent physical conditions. When your doctor prescribes a drug, does he or she warn you of the side effects? If not, be sure to ask. Always be sure to read the labels for any medication you take.

The real speed limit is an invisible one. The real speed trap is the failure to adjust speed for the conditions.

SUGGESTED PRACTICE ACTIVITIES

For each of the cases, judge when and where a probable conflict will occur. Then, choose the best change of speed such as: (a) no change, (b) gradual increase, (c) quick increase, (d) gradual decrease, and (e) quick decrease. Also, choose the best path.

1. Case of the Blind Spot Driver

You are driving car "A" on a freeway in the blind spot of car "B". Car "C" is speeding up to merge. Car "B" has signaled and started to drift toward lane line.

2. Case of the Right Side Passer

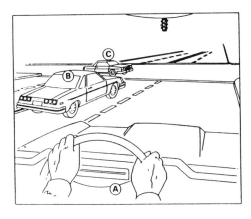

You are driving car "A" as the signal turns green. Car "B" is slow to move, so you start to pass. As you reach the corner, car "C" is trying to beat the light change.

3. Case of the Hidden Bike

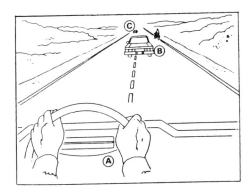

You are in car "A" and starting to pass "B" since "C" a safe distance away. Just then, "B" moves across center line. You know why when you see the bike.

4. Case of the Sports Car Passer

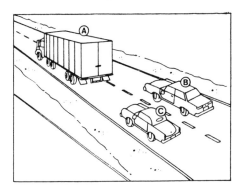

You are driving "B" on a freeway and just been passed by truck "A". Then you see sports car starting to pass. What can you expect? Assume you are the truck driver.

5. Case of the Hillcrest Hazard

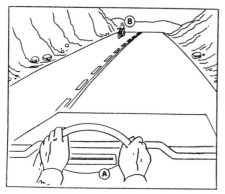

You are driving "A" about 55 mph on a rural highway. When you are about four seconds from the hillcrest, a bike "B" appears over the hill. The shoulders are narrow.

6. Case of the Crossover

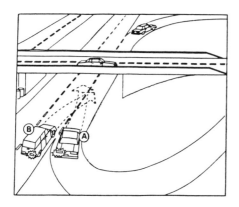

At a cloverleaf interchange, you are in car "A" ready to merge. Car "B" signals and starts to slow down for an exit.

Note: This is probably the most critical positioning and timing problem on the interstate highways. What general rules would you suggest for cars "A" and "B" to follow?

CHAPTER 9
RESPONDING TO CRITICAL SITUATIONS

As a driver, you will face critical situations from time to time. This is because machines have failures and drivers make errors. Such situations happen suddenly with little warning and can cause panic to the unprepared. They require quick and proper responses if collisions are to be avoided or minimized. So, the key to the correct responses is proper preparation.

This chapter will provide a knowledge of what to do in most emergencies. The focus is on programming the mind rather than advanced physical skills. A high degree of physical training usually deteriorates when not used regularly. Some practice in simulated situations can help build up your confidence.

GENERAL GUIDELINES

There are a number of mental and physical habits you can develop in normal driving situations. After all, many of the critical situations are the result of complex situations that get out of control.

Schedule Proper Maintenance

Always keep your car in safe operating condition. Follow the owner's manual for routine preventive maintenance. Keep tires properly inflated.

Plan to See and Be Seen

Low-beam headlights should be used in the daytime when visibility is poor. Horns should be used to warn of trouble or one's presence. A car that must be parked on the shoulder needs to be protected with the flasher lights and other approved methods. At night, turn on the dome light.

Test Slippery Surfaces

A change in weather conditions may make the road surface more slippery than you realize. You can test the surface conditions by going slow in an area free of traffic. Then apply the brakes to see if the tires start to slide. Accelerate to find out if the drive wheels start to spin. Adjust your speed to the conditions noted.

Steering is Lost When Brakes Are Locked

On cars without anti-lock brakes, the tires will start sliding when the brake pedal is held down at high speed. When the brakes are locked, the sliding front wheels can still be turned, but there will be no change in direction.

Locked Brakes Take Longer to Stop

Once the brakes are locked, no additional braking effect can be produced. On cars without anti-lock brakes, the best method for stopping is to apply the brakes just short of the lock-up. Then, ease up and apply a squeezing action to the brake pedal. Such controlled braking helps prevent skidding and allows the wheels to be steered. On snow packed roads, this allows the snow to drop out of the tread for better traction.

Swerving Distance is Less Than Stopping Distance

At speeds above 30 mph, the distance required to steer around an object is less than the distance it takes to stop before hitting that object. The hands are quicker than the feet. Usually less traction is required to steer than to stop.

Develop the Cover Brake Habit

When coming to an intersection or other area of probable conflict, use the cover brake habit. This action involves placing the foot over the brake pedal with no pressure on the brakes. Such action provides for readiness to act and less reaction time.

Go For the Soft Landing

If a collision can't be avoided, you should steer toward an object that will have the least resistance. Bushes, snow banks, fences, or embankments should be selected. If a solid object must be hit, then hit it a glancing blow rather than head on. Try never to give up steering for the best pathway.

Mentally Rehearse Plans As You Drive

Fortunately, emergencies do not happen very often. Unfortunately, this makes it hard to remember the correct response when one does happen. So, you need to use routine situations for mental rehearsal. For example, when the shoulder is observed to be lower than the pavement, remind yourself of the proper steps for the off-road recovery. When approaching a problem situation, remember to look for an escape path along with the steps for using it. This helps you keep alert and prepared. Also, it builds up self-confidence in your ability to avoid collisions.

OFF-ROAD RECOVERY

You may go off the roadway onto the shoulder on purpose or accidentally. How you get back onto the pavement is the critical part. The problem increases when the edge of the pavement is two or more inches higher than the surface of the shoulder. If you panic and turn quickly at high speed against this edge, you can lose control and go across the road into other traffic. If you brake suddenly with two wheels on the soft shoulder and two wheels on the pavement, your car will probably start skidding out of control. You can prevent any loss of control by using these steps.

Center Steer

As soon as the two outside wheels drop off the edge of the pavement, steer straight ahead parallel with the edge. Stay calm and keep a firm grip on the steering wheel. A real soft or wet shoulder could pull your car into the ditch.

Slow Down Gradually

Let up on the gas pedal to slow down. Do not use the brakes unless you are headed for a concrete bridge abutment or other fixed object. If you must brake, use controlled braking so you can steer. Slow down to about 35 mph.

Signal and Turn Onto Pavement

Check traffic and signal. Steer about one-fourth turn onto the pavement. Straighten into the first lane and speed up to flow of traffic. Power steering will make this less of a steering problem.

EVASIVE MANEUVERS

The most serious errors by other drivers are those which cause their vehicles to enter your immediate pathway ahead. Of course, you too can misjudge a situation and end up with a serious conflict. In such cases you will need to make quick changes in your car speed and direction. They are like a quick change of lanes. Involved are swerving and controlled braking or rapid acceleration. The combination of these actions results in an evasive maneuver. Following are steps to take for such actions.

Blow Horn and Flash Lights

The other driver or pedestrian may be inattentive, tired or under the influence of drugs. So a blast of the horn and/or flashing of the headlights may help.

Controlled Braking

The purpose of controlled braking is to slow down quickly without losing steering ability. Then, swerving can be done when required. Such braking is done by squeezing on the brake pedal until the wheels start to lock. Then, release the pressure and squeeze again and again. Do not make the release with the anti-lock braking system.

Rapid Acceleration

There will be times when you will want to use rapid acceleration to get out of a tight situation. This can happen in passing situations or when other vehicles are closing in on your pathway from the side. Merging onto a freeway usually calls for various amounts of acceleration.

Rapid acceleration involves a quick push of the gas pedal all the way to the floor when driving an automatic transmission car. On cars with a clutch, you should downshift before pushing on the gas pedal to provide for quicker pick-up in speed. Check the owner's manual for the proper procedure to follow for your car model.

Swerve Right or Left

Swerving requires that you turn the steering wheel quickly at least one-half turn in the desired direction. After clearing an object, turn the steering wheel almost a full circle in the opposite direction. Finally, return to center steering if you wish to keep moving along your intended path of travel.

SKID CONTROL ACTIONS

Skidding is the sliding or spinning of the tires on the roadway surface. This results in temporary loss of control, since a sliding or spinning wheel cannot be steered. Skidding is due to improper driver actions for the roadway conditions.

Braking Skids

Skids can be caused when you push the brake pedal too hard on a slippery surface. As soon as you feel the tires start to slide, release the pressure on the brakes. Then, apply pressure as needed. Downshifting to low can help a car slow down.

Power Skids

When you accelerate too quickly or too much on a slippery surface, the drive wheels begin spinning. Usually, one end of the car will fishtail or slide sideways. To gain control of a power skid, release the pressure on the gas pedal.

Power skids are most apt to happen when you accelerate going up a slippery hill. The best way to prevent such a skid is to build up momentum before reaching the hill. Then, you may need only steady pressure on the gas pedal to climb the hill.

Cornering Skids

These are skids in which the rear end of the car slides sideways. They are usually caused by going around a corner too fast. Braking or accelerating part way around a curve or corner also can produce such a skid.

To recover from a cornering skid, you should let up on the gas pedal and steer toward the intended pathway. Do not brake. Your first steering action will usually be too much. So, always be ready to make quick but slight steering movements in the opposite direction to correct for oversteering. It will take some skill to keep the car from skidding out of control.

BRAKE FAILURES

Properly maintained brakes seldom fail. If a drive belt breaks or the engine stalls, the power unit will no longer assist you. Wet brakes may not stop the car at all. Loss of brake fluid can cause the system to fail completely.

Power Assist Fails

The brakes will still slow or stop the car. All you need to do is use more pressure on the pedal.

Wet Brakes

After driving through deep water for some distance, brake linings can become soaked and may no longer stop the car. Test them to see if they work. If they do not work properly, turn onto the shoulder or into a parking lot. Then, press the brake pedal down with your left foot as you move forward and backward slowly. The heat from the friction should soon dry out the lining.

Brake Fade

Excesssive use of the brakes on a steep downgrade can cause brake linings to overheat and result in fading. Pull off the roadway and stop as soon as possible. Let the brakes cool off. Then test for proper functioning. At the first opportunity, have the brakes checked for permanent damage.

Complete Loss of Brakes

If the brakes do not hold at all, warn others by blowing the horn and turning on the four-way flashers. Then, pump the brake pedal rapidly. If some pressure returns, pull off the road and park. If no pressure, shift to low and let up on the gas pedal. Then turn off the ignition. Try using the park brake. As a last resort, steer up a hill or an embankment. If there is no hill, rub tires along a curb or sideswipe something.

SUGGESTED PRACTICE ACTIVITIES

1. Select a level stretch of rural highway with wide shoulders that are lower than the pavement. Then, practice slipping off of the pavement with only two wheels onto the shoulder. Practice at speeds of 30,40, and 50 mph until you feel comfortable pulling partway onto a shoulder and returning back onto the first lane of the pavement.

2. On vacant parking lots and then stretches of a freeway, practice rapid acceleration and controlled hard braking at various speeds. This is especially important when you buy your first car with the anti-lock brakes (ABS).

3. When the roadways become slippery, practice corner-skids on vacant parking lots. In hilly areas, practice accelerating uphill and braking downhill.

For each of the cases illustrated, choose (a) the best position, (b) the best speed adjustment, and (c) the best communication. Compare your evaluations and the responses with a relative or friend.

4. Case of the Merge Conflict

You are driving "A" on a divided highway. As you come to a merging area, "B" swerves into your lane within the four second stopping zone. What are options, with or without a following vehicle?

5. Case of the Follow-Tail Passer

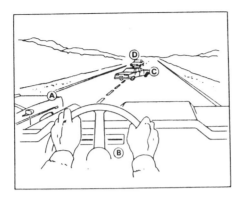

You are driving car "A" and following car "C" around car "B" on a two-lane highway. The front of your car is almost even with the front of "B". Then you realize car "D" is closer than you thought.

What is your best option? If you slow down to cut back behind "B" and car "B" slows down at the same time to help out, nothing is gained. The general rule for driver "B" is to maintain speed and let the passing driver make the first move. If driver "A" speeds up, then "B" can slow down.

6. Case of the Slow Starter

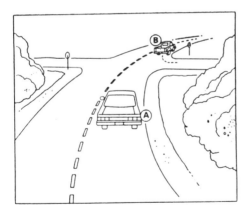

You are driving car "A" about 55 mph on a two-lane highway that curves to right just ahead of a side road that is partly hidden. Truck "B" turns on to highway. You will not have the distance to stop before hitting "B".

What are the options? Compare a probable head on collision with hitting the rear of pick-up or taking the ditch. Assume you a driver "B". After hearing a horn and checking the mirror, what would you do?

7. Case of the Oncoming Passer

You are driver "A" on a two-lane road. Car "B" has passed "D" and car "C" is also trying to pass car "D". You are faced with a good chance of a head on crash.

Try to check out the front wheels of car "C". You would not want to steer onto the shoulder at the same time as car "C" did. In a real case, the two cars met head on in the ditch. A mother and her two children were killed.

If both you and and car "D" give some to the right, then car "C" may be able to squeeze by down the middle.

CHAPTER 10
MANAGING DRIVER RISKS

We all take risks every day. Whether we are doing something at home, working or driving, there is always the chance that our actions may result in some loss. The risks involved in driving can result in injury and even death. Therefore, we must learn how to manage driver risks in a way that can reduce to a minimum the chances for such serious losses.

Risk taking exists in human activities because there is uncertainty about what is about to happen. If we could be certain of what will happen in the future, we could easily predict the safest actions to take. The behavior of another driver or pedestrian may be predicted, based on traffic laws and our experience, but we cannot know for sure.

Risk taking consists of a driver voluntarily entering a situation in which there is a source of danger. So, drivers will constantly be involved in judging the nature and seriousness of such dangers. They can then choose the best response to make. Since it is the behavior of the driver that is the risk rather than the situation, risk taking is a part of the decision-making process. Our objective, then, is to learn how to make choices with the least chance of loss.

Since risk taking is a part of the decision-making process, the probability of a collision depends on the degree or level of risk that a driver decides to accept. The level of risk can be judged by perceiving the probability for a collision to happen. Then, there is also the need to judge the seriousness of the loss. The higher the level of risk accepted, the greater the exposure to serious dangers.

Low level or normal risks are those in which there is little or no chance of a conflict occurring. If a conflict did occur, then the consequences would be negligible, and the benefits would outweigh the losses. For example, when following another motor vehicle, the driver decides to maintain a distance of at least two seconds from the car ahead. Drivers can accept such low levels of risk and still be relatively safe.

A high level of risk is one in which a driver takes a course of action that does not allow for the normal margin of safety. An example would be when a driver tailgates another motor vehicle at a high rate of speed. Such high risks are unnecessary and actually foolish because the chance for serious loss always outweighs the chance for a small gain. It is the high level risks that we can and must manage if we are to become safe and efficient drivers.

WHY DRIVERS TAKE HIGH RISKS

Why do drivers take high risks when, statistically, there is such a high probability of serious loss? An understanding of why so many of us do take high risks can help us avoid and manage such risks.

The Need to Save Time

Although the modern automobile has given us the fastest mode of personal travel on land, there still seems to be the need to save more time. Drivers may be in a hurry to get to an important appointment or just to get home. They become impatient with the other drivers, exceed the speed limit, and take higher risks than usual.

In addition to speeding, the driver in a hurry is more apt to pass with little margin of safety and cut off another driver. They will tend to accept a smaller time-space gap for completing other maneuvers. Once they get by with such behavior, it is easier to develop these risky behaviors into habits. What most of these drivers do not realize is that little time is saved.

The Effect of Emotions on Risk-Taking

Emotions are a normal part of life just as risks are. As emotional creatures, it is only natural that we attach meaning and feeling to what we do. This means that our decisions are not necessarily based on rational or objective thought processes. So, emotions may influence the degree of risk a driver is willing to take at any given time. The stronger the response the more effect it can have on risk-taking. And, no one is free from emotional upsets or strong feelings.

Any number of situations can lead to temporary upsets. One person may have had a frightening experience at home or at work. Another may have just received news of a serious illness in the family. Then, there is the person who has had a serious argument, jumps in his car, and drives off mad.

Many situations that arise in traffic may also lead to strong emotions. A driver jumps the green light or another cuts in front of a car when passing. It is easy to become angry at these kinds of drivers. Also, one can become frustrated or impatient while waiting in long lines of traffic. Then there are those who do not signal their intentions.

The Effects of Alcohol on Risk-Taking

Mixing alcohol and driving is one of the highest risks drivers can take. About one-half of the fatal automobile collisions involve a driver who has been drinking. Intoxicated drivers are also involved in a significant number of non-fatal collisions.

Alcohol is a depressant drug that affects a driver's vision, judgment, and reaction time. A sober driver takes about three/fourths second to react and apply the controls. The driver with at least two drinks will need double the reaction time. The reason more impaired drivers do not have collisions is because there is low traffic density late at night.

A "hangover" may appear after most of the alcohol has left the body and the person awakens from sleep. During a "hangover" the person may have a headache, an upset stomach, blurred vision, and slowed reaction. Therefore, a person can still be unfit to drive during this time period.

Inefficient Visual Skills

Finally, many drivers may fail to perceive high level risks due to ignorance, inexperience, or poor visual skills. We know that beginning drivers cannot acquire adequate perceptual skills in the short courses now being provided. Most young people receive only six hours of behind-the-wheel instruction which is usually just enough to pass the easy state road test.

The inexperienced or those who have not developed adequate perceptual skills are easily distracted and become inattentive from time to time. When they do observe a danger, it may be too late to respond properly. They may concentrate on one danger and fail to perceive another.

HOW TO AVOID AND MINIMIZE HIGH RISKS

Driver risks can be managed through knowledge and training. Managing driver risks is the process of planing and taking necessary actions not only to prevent collisions, but to minimize the impact of loss should such an unfortunate incident occur.

Exposure to dangers does not need to be a high risk. It does not mean one has to gamble or take undue chances. The great majority of driver risks are not hidden or unexpected. When an acceptable margin of safety is maintained, risk can easily be controlled by the perceptive and responsible driver. Then, we can have confidence in being a lifetime safe driver.

Few things in driving happen without any advance warning. The competent driver has a general plan or strategy for dealing with the various kinds of events.

As a perceptive driver, you will not be surprised by rapidly changing events or probable conflicts that can trap you into a high risk situation.

Identify and Assess the Level of Risk

To keep risk under control, we must first be able to identify the risk ahead, then assess the level of the risk. Our objective is to separate the routine choices or low risks from the critical decisions or high risks. High risks, such as passing on a hill or driving under the influence of alcohol, can then be considered as unacceptable.

A main purpose of this book is to help you improve those selective perceptual skills that will enable you to identify high risks in time to make wise decisions.

Avoid Some Risks with Preventive Maintenance

Cars that do not function properly not only increase the level of risk, but they increase operating costs as well. When you want to pass on a two-lane highway or accelerate onto a freeway, you want the engine to respond promptly with no sputtering or missing. The brakes must be operating properly for any quick stop or emergency.

You can avoid such risks by following the preventive maintenance schedules listed in your owner manual. Preventive maintenance is a plan for inspecting a car thoroughly and systematically at regular intervals. Besides performing any required services, mechanics can catch any signs of wear or damage before they can cause a breakdown. It will ensure that your car warranty will not be adversely affected.

In addition to professional inspections, there are a number of ones you should make regularly. As you walk to your parked car, get into the habit of looking around and under the car. Note the color of any liquid leaks from the radiator that is yellowish-green.

A reddish color is from the transmission or power steering, and black or dark brown is oil from the engine. Clear water is from the air conditioner.

Inspect the tires for cuts, objects in the tread, and sidewall cracks. Look for uneven wear and inflation. Properly inflated tires give up to five percent better gas mileage. Improperly inflated tires result in abnormal wear and lessened handling ability. Check the air pressure at least once a month when cold.

Check the lights to see if they need cleaning. At least once a month, have someone turn on each set of lights while you observe them. Then, when your car is facing the garage door, turn on the headlamps. Switch from low beam to high beam to check for the proper alignment

You should do a few under-the-hood checks every other time you fill up with gasoline at a self-service pump. They are easy to do and should always be made before starting on a long trip. Review your owner's manual to guide such inspections.

In addition to such regular inspections, you will need to recognize any abnormal sounds and odors. These are usually an early warning of a problem that needs prompt attention. So, report and describe as best you can to the service manager or mechanic.

Minimize Some Risks by Smart Trip Planning

Preparing for trips and selecting the best routes can help you avoid some risks and minimize those that cannot be avoided. For both short and long trips, it is best to have one or two alternate routes. Then, in case of road repairs, bad weather or heavy traffic, you are prepared. Route selection can save fuel and time as well as reduce the risks.

Usually, the best routes are selected on the basis of time rather that the miles traveled. Then, you can choose the best time to start. In cities and suburbs, try to pick routes that have the fewest stop situations. Stop and go situations increase the chances for rear collisions and use more gasoline. Also, they cause more wear on the tires and brakes. When the pavement is slick, try to pick a route with the fewest stops at the top or bottom of hills. It is also best to choose routes with the fewest left turns against traffic unless such turns are protected by controls.

On long trips, select and mark the best routes to follow based on road design features and surface conditions. Once you have marked your maps, make out a log for the trip. For each leg, record the mileage, average speed, travel time and time for stops. Using this log, you can figure the total miles and travel time for the complete trip. This provides an estimate of the total costs and the best time to start.

Before starting a long trip, make sure you get a good night's rest. Staying up late to pack and load a car is not wise. Fix in your mind the first leg of the trip to be followed. If small children are to be included, make sure you take some games, books and toys. Older children may learn to read the map and help remember the route changes. They should be able to calculate the average miles per gallon of gasoline and the costs.

Minimize Risks by Maintaining a Margin of Safety

The best and safest drivers are the smoothest. Everything they do looks easy. This is because they have learned how to maintain an adequate margin of safety. Such a margin gives them plenty of space and time to respond to changing conditions. It also gives them better visibility. So, they minimize the risks and rarely need to make sudden stops or swerving actions.

In heavy traffic or on narrow highways, you may not be able to maintain adequate space margins to the sides. You can't control road conditions or other user movements, but you can control where to meet other users by timing. So, proper timing of your vehicle movements, by adjusting speed, is an essential part of maintaining a proper safety margin. Chapter Eight provided you with the principles to follow for timing your actions.

It is obvious that choosing an adequate safety margin involves managing the space and time available for perceiving, deciding, and making proper responses. It is done by choosing the best speed and position for your vehicle. The amount needed will vary with the speed at the time of the planned actions needed. It will also vary with the weather, traffic conditions and the type of highway.

Avoid Some Risks by Controlling Emotions

Our strong emotions can be controlled if we under-stand how our brain processes information and makes driving judgments. For our purposes, the brain can be divided into four main parts: (1) the forebrain, (2) the midbrain, (3) hindbrain, and (4) the lower brain stem.

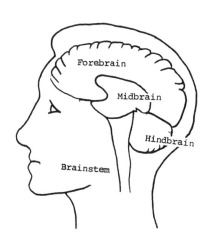

The forebrain (cerebrum) contains millions of tiny cells, some of which are commonly referred to as gray matter. This part receives and acts upon the sensations of vision, smell, hearing, taste and touch. Here is located the center of thought, reason, and judgment. When this part of the brain is not properly functioning, a person is said to have lost control.

The midbrain consists of the upper part of the brainstem and surrounding groups of cells. It contains the main nerve pathways. One area of the midbrain serves as a relay station, and is like a telephone switchboard. It sorts and chooses between important and unimportant sensory messages. Some messages are put through to the forebrain immediately for processing, and others are relayed to the hindbrain. Still others may be changed or screened out.

The midbrain is also the center of our emotions. Here is where our feelings about things develop. It triggers feelings of fear, anger, anxiety, etc. This part helps us run from danger, seek out exiting things to do, and fight for what we believe. This is why emotions can play a significant role in the total brain action and hence influence our behavior as a driver.

The hindbrain (cerebellum) is located behind and below the rest of the brain. Its main function is to control and coordinate the work of the muscular system. Most of this work is done automatically. The hindbrain also helps us maintain balance and posture.

Because the messages to and from the higher centers of the brain must pass through the center of emotions, they are subject to possible changes and interpretations. So, a driver's normal responses to common traffic situations can change a lot when he or she is emotionally upset. To the degree that a strong emotion can overcome reason, we can lose our ability to see things clearly, to decide wisely, and to perform skillfully.

Fortunately, we are not born with strong emotions. The way we respond emotionally is learned as we grow up. For example, we learn what to get angry about and what situations to worry about. We learn what experiences help us feel joyful. Since strong emotions are learned, we can change and control them. The following guidelines should help you keep emotions from unduly affecting your driving abilities.

Understand your own emotional makeup. The more we know why we act a certain way, the better we can control ourselves and enjoy life. If we can admit when we are angry or frustrated and accept these feelings in ourselves, then we have a better chance of keeping them under control. A small amount of anger may be a health outlet. Emotions that are bottled up for any length of time are more apt to explode into upsets. When you have a strong emotion that will interfere with driving and you know it, then you can do something about it.

Identify situations that can lead to upsets. Whether or not a situation arouses a strong emotion depends upon its importance and one's ability to cope with it. We tend to be afraid or angry when we are faced with conflicts and threatening situations. If we can foresee situations that could lead easily to upsets, then we can prepare for them. One way is to have a mind-set in advance on how to handle such situations. We can avoid many problem traffic situations by good trip planning.

Expect drivers to make mistakes and have upsets. The more we drive, the more we realize that all of us are going to make mistakes. There will be times when we as well as others may be inattentive or distracted. Some persons may not have the knowledge or skills they should have. Remember, too, that emotions can be contagious. So, don't let the foolish acts of another driver trap you into doing something just as bad. Realize that smiles and courtesy can be spread among drivers just as easily as upsets.

Direct emotions to acts of people not the people. It is easy to get mad at another person or driver without knowing exactly why. If we are not careful, we will start thinking that other drivers are trying to take advantage of us. Remember, the other driver does not know you or have anything against you. So, concentrate on what the other user does rather than what kind of person you think he or she is.

Delay driving when you are upset. Most emotional upsets are temporary. So, if you have to drive, it is best to wait until the strength of the emotion wears down and reaches a safe level. When the upset happens while driving, find a place to park and relax. Take a short walk around the car and check it over.

You may use the time to stop for refreshments.

Some persons actually think it is a good idea to drive around to "cool off" when upset. Of course, this is a very mistaken idea. We should never be tempted to use the car to escape from reality, to show off, or to get even. Walking, hiking or playing a game are more sensible things to do.

Avoid Some Risks by Controlling the Use of Alcohol

Years ago, a noted humorist said: "Ignorance is not so much a lack of knowledge, but that people know so many things that ain't so." When it comes to controlling the effects of an alcoholic beverage on the body, some people still believe the folklore that they can sober up by exercising, drinking black coffee, or taking a cold shower. Such folklore just ain't so.

As a driver, pedestrian and passenger, you will have to deal with the drinking-driving problem whether or not you choose to use alcoholic beverages. Today, most licensed drivers in the United States also drink to some extent. You can help reduce the high risks associated with driving and drinking by adopting a strict set of personal guidelines. It won't be easy, but it is the best way to reduce and control the problem.

Know why people choose to drink. Alcohol is one of the oldest commonly use drugs. Traditionally, many people have used alcoholic beverages for social, dietary and ceremonial reasons. Some people seem to enjoy having a drink along with good food and good friends. They find a moderate amount to be relaxing.

There is no doubt that many young people begin drinking because their parents drink, especially at meals. Adolescents are also influenced by peer pressure at parties. Add boredom to the feelings of low self-esteem, and alcohol can easily become a way to escape reality. Then there are the million dollar advertisements.

When people drink to drink rather than to socialize, they are on their way to becoming a problem drinker. A signal for becoming dependent or addicted to alcohol is when a person starts drinking alone at home and at a bar. This is when family members or friends should suggest professional advice be sought. Alcoholism is a common but complex health problem and needs to be treated as promptly as any other disease.

Know what you and others are drinking. The percentage of alcohol in the bloodstream at any one time determines whether or not a driver's abilities are impaired. To keep this blood-alcohol-concentration (BAC) to a minimum, the drinker must know the amount of alcohol in the various drinks. The amount in each standard "drink" is easy to remember. A one ounce jigger of whiskey, a four ounce glass of wine, or a twelve ounce bottle (can) of beer all contain about one-half ounce of alcohol. Beware of and question the amount in unfamiliar drinks. To be safe, always overestimate the amount of alcohol in mixed drinks and fortified wine.

To estimate the actual percentage of alcohol that is absorbed into the bloodstream, you will need to know the person's weight. For a one hundred pound person, one "drink" of beer, wine, or whiskey will usually produce a BAC of about 0.04. The same "drink" will produce only 0.02 BAC in a two hundred pound person.

Recognize time as a key factor in the content of the BAC. Alcohol is absorbed directly into the bloodstream through the lining of the stomach and the intestines. It takes less than two minutes for some of the alcohol to reach the higher centers of the brain. How quickly the rest of the drink will be absorbed and reach the forebrain depends on the (a) rate of drinking, (b) kind of beverage, and (c) food in the stomach.

If persons take their time and sip rather than gulp down a drink, they give the body a better chance to handle the alcohol. Eating before and while drinking can slow the absorption rate by as much as one-third. Foods high in protein and starch are best for this purpose. Beer and wine usually take longer to drink and they do have some food content.

The body gets rid of alcohol through oxidation and elimination. Oxidation is simply the burning of alcohol by the liver. The liver can burn up about one-half ounce of alcohol in one hour. Some people falsely believe they can speed up this process which gets rid of ninety percent of the alcohol consumed. They cannot.

Only a small amount of alcohol is eliminated from the body through the lungs, perspiration and urine. Some people who drink beer and urinate frequently may assume the beer is going through the body with little effect. Actually, it is only excess water that is being eliminated, not the alcohol.

So, time is the key factor. If a person of average weight allows one hour for each drink, he or she can remain relatively sober. Those who consume more than one drink each hour will become intoxicated to some extent.

Plan to set limits in advance. The highest center of the forebrain is affected first by alcohol consumption. This means the lack of some self-criticism may not be realized by the drinker. By the second drink within an hour, judgment is beginning to be impaired enough to make it difficult to decide when to stop drinking. So, there is a need to pick the number and kind of drinks to consume ahead of time. This mental set ahead of time will help people stick to a plan.

After the second or third drink within an hour, the midbrain is affected. The result can be emotional instability, loss of memory and less ability to concentrate. Then a person will have difficulty deciding not to take a fourth drink.

The person who is tired or depressed should recall that alcohol is a depressant drug. So, that person has two things that will slow him or her down. Also, some drugs, combined with alcohol, can produce the effects that are greater than the sum of each. For example, when alcohol is added to a barbituate, the effect can be multiplied three or four times. The abuse of alcohol and sleeping pills has caused many deaths.

When one sets a limit as to the number of drinks to have during a period of time and when to stop drinking before driving, then the BAC can be fairly well controlled. It is best to switch early to some-thing else and get more involved in social activities. People need to be honest with themselves and realize it doesn't take much alcohol to serve ceremonial and social needs. They will not try to keep up with the others or let friends push another unwanted drink.

Be a responsible host or hostess. It is a moral and sometimes legal responsibility for hosts or hostesses at gatherings to see that their guests do not drive if in-toxicated. They can plan interesting activities and have a tempting display of food or snacks available. They should always have non-alcoholic drinks available, and about an hour before the event ends, stop serving the alcoholic beverages.

SOME AFTERTHOUGHTS

We hope some of the ideas and guidelines for im-proving your perceptual driving skills have been helpful to you. Still, you may be thinking, "Who in the world has time to do all that while driving?" You're right; it is a lot to ask. However, let's not forget the power of the human brain.

The human brain is like a giant computer. With practice, it will be able to process most data within a fraction of a second. But, like a computer, the brain is of little value if it hasn't been given the right kind of information. It will also need some rules or guidelines for using the information it is storing away. This is what we have been trying to present to you--both the best kind of information and the guidelines for applying it.

At one time or another, you have probably solved a puzzle. What happens the second time you try to solve it? It seems much easier, and it takes only a fraction of the time it did the first time. This is because you can identify the clues more quickly, and you know what to expect. You no longer have to rely on trial and error. Then too, similar puzzles become easier to work, even on the first try.

This same puzzle-solving principle applies to coping with traffic situations. As you continue to practice your improved mental skills in a vehicle as a driver or as a passenger, you will be able to handle the common situations almost automatically. This will free the higher centers of your brain to deal properly with the unusual or more complex traffic situations. As these mental skills continue to improve, the chances of you getting trapped into a collision course will become less and less.

Another interesting thing will begin to happen, too. Your brain will bring together all you have experienced into one whole process. Your eye habits, your identification and evaluation abilities, and the information you have stored will all combine into one single set of mental skills. As you scan the traffic scene, you will quickly perceive the probable conflicts and decide how to respond. This will increase your confidence, and then, as you look back on your driving experiences, you will take pride in your ability to drive without ever having a preventable collision.

Good luck!